Lake District

Car Tours

Anne-Marie Edwards

Acknowledgements

I would like to thank the staff of the Lake District Information Centres at Windermere, Keswick and Ambleside for their friendly help and advice in the planning of this book. Among the many people who helped us on our way I am particularly grateful to Revd Chris Cowper for his valuable information about Bridekirk. Thanks also go to Mr and Mrs M. R. Smith and to the staff at Southampton and Totton libraries for all their help. I am grateful to Heather Pearson, Sandy Sims and other members of the staff at the Ordnance Survey, Southampton, for their patient assistance. Finally, I thank my husband Mike who accompanied me.

Front cover photograph: *Ashness Bridge*
Title page photograph: *View westwards from Side Pike, Great Langdale*

Author and Series Editor: Anne-Marie Edwards
Editor: Paula Granados
Designers: Brian Skinner, Doug Whitworth
Photographs: Mike Edwards and Jarrold Publishing

Ordnance Survey   ISBN 0-3190-0490-2
Jarrold Publishing   ISBN 0-7117-0823-1

First published 1995 by Ordnance Survey and Jarrold Publishing

Ordnance Survey   Jarrold Publishing
Romsey Road   Whitefriars
Maybush   Norwich NR3 1TR
Southampton SO16 4GU

© Ordnance Survey and Jarrold Publishing 1995
Maps © Crown copyright 1995

Printed in Great Britain by Jarrold Printing, Norwich. 1/95

CONTENTS

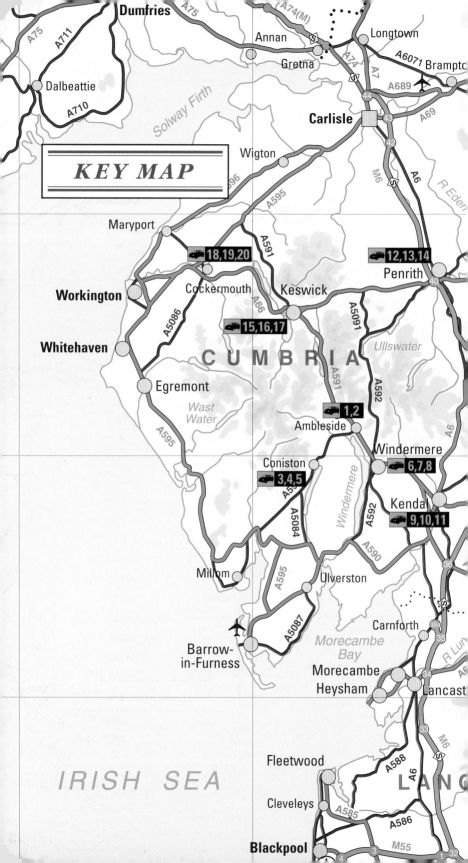

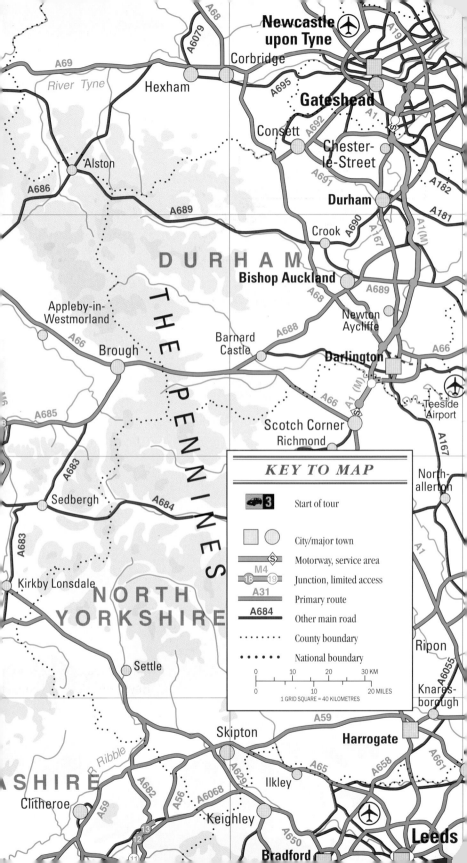

Newcastle upon Tyne ✈

A68

A6079

Corbridge

River Tyne

Hexham

A69

A695

Gateshead

A692

Consett

A1

Chester-le-Street

A691

A686

Alston

A689

Durham

A690

A167

A181

A182

A1(M)

Crook

D U R H A M

Bishop Auckland

A68

A689

Newton Aycliffe

A66

Appleby-in-Westmorland

A66

Brough

Barnard Castle

A688

T H E

Darlington

Teeside Airport ✈

A685

A6

A685

A683

A1 (M)

A66

Sedbergh

A684

P E N N I N E S

Scotch Corner

Richmond

A167

North-allerton

A683

Kirkby Lonsdale

N O R T H

Y O R K S H I R E

A1

Settle

Ripon

A6055

Knaresborough

A59

Skipton

Harrogate

R. Ribble

A629

A65

A658

A661

A682

Ilkley

SHIRE

Clitheroe

A59

A56

A6068

Keighley

13

12

A650

Bradford

11

Leeds

✈

INTRODUCTION TO
THE LAKE DISTRICT

I<small>N</small> the spring of 1794 Dorothy Wordsworth, with her brother
William by her side, walked across the Lake District from Kendal
to Keswick. She was entranced by the beauty of the landscape.
She wrote to a friend that they walked 'through the most delightful
country that ever was seen'. Today, over two hundred years later, the
Lake District continues to enchant all who see it. Part of its charm
must lie in its compactness. Tucked away in the north-west corner
of Cumbria, the Lake District National Park is a mere 30 miles across,
but so diverse is the scenery that it feels much larger. Its boundaries
are clearly defined: to the west by the sea and to the north by the
Solway plains. Southwards it is fringed by the sands of Morecambe
Bay and eastwards it is distanced from the Pennine chain by the Eden
valley. From whatever direction they are approached the dark curves
of the lakeland peaks rise outlined against the sky hinting at a secret
kingdom waiting to be explored.

The Lake District never disappoints the fourteen million or so
visitors who arrive each year. Here is a magical blend of lakes and
rivers each with its own special appeal, open fells laced with dry-
stone walls and wooded valleys dotted with long, low farmhouses
surrounded by brilliant green fields. Deer roam the more remote
fells and forests, red squirrels can be seen in the woods, the lakes
provide a haven for waterfowl, and eagles soar above the highest

*Sheer cliffs guard the
southern approach of
St Johns in the Vale*

An old house in Hartsop which has retained its balustraded spinning gallery

crags. But it is not only nature's world. An often turbulent history is reflected in the many peel towers, built as places of refuge, and the great houses and castles that ring the central fells. Throughout the area are many fascinating places to visit illustrating the character, occupations and traditions of the independent lakeland people.

Another of the secrets of the Lake District's lasting hold over its visitors is that there is always more to discover. The structure of the landscape, affected by the nature of the underlying rocks, glaciation and erosion, is so complicated that it is almost impossible to feel one has seen it all! The best way to grasp an overall picture of the area is to adopt the plan proposed by Wordsworth in his *Guide to the Lakes* and imagine oneself looking down on the mountains from a central position between Great Gable and Scafell. The lakeland valleys then appear to radiate outwards like the spokes of a wheel from the highest mountains in the centre. But, as Wordsworth says, this pattern is only a broad outline, within it lies an infinite variety of intermediate valleys, rocky ridges, corries and fells.

This complex landscape owes its origin in the first place to the nature of the rock. Travelling from north to south you see quite dramatic changes in scenery from the rounded, dome-shaped slopes of Skiddaw above Keswick, through the high craggy peaks of central lakeland, such as the Langdale Pikes and the Scafell Range, to the low, well-wooded fells surrounding Windermere and the southern valleys. The oldest rocks are in the north, the Skiddaw Slates, formed about five hundred million years ago from layers of mud and clay. Later volcanic disturbance formed the very hard rocks in the centre known as Borrowdale Volcanics. About four hundred million years ago the land was covered by the sea which receded leaving behind a rich deposit of silt. This formed soft rocks known as Silurian Grits, easily eroded and fertile, covering southern lakeland. Later, deposits of shells created a canopy of limestone which was shaken off

*View over Lake
Windermere from
Gummers How*

outwards when the land was lifted out of the sea again. Horizontal
limestone slabs can be seen today around Kendal. During a period
of very hot conditions abrasive sand, reddened with iron, filled the
valleys beyond the limestone ring creating the beautiful sandstone
used to build the villages around Penrith and in the Eden valley.

But the landscape we recognise today was shaped by ice. At
the height of the Ice Age, some two million years ago, it is possible
the whole area was covered by a dome of ice. By the end of the last
Ice Age, some ten thousand years ago, the weight of the ice and the
advance downhill of glaciers had scoured deep U-shaped valleys and
transported fragments of mountainside, known as glacial erratics, to
be deposited many miles away. Melting ice formed lakes and tarns.

Man has also left his mark. Working with stone axes quarried from
hard volcanic rocks, New Stone Age farmers gradually cleared most
of the pines from the upper mountain slopes and many of the oaks
from the lower fells. Men of the ensuing Bronze Age erected the
great stone circles, notably Castlerigg near Keswick and Long Meg
and her Daughters near Little Salkeld, which still puzzle us today. The
Romans, troubled by rebellious Celtic tribes, have left the remains of
their great wall stretching from the Solway Firth east through Carlisle,
the routes of their roads, and the foundations of many forts, the most

The Victorian Steam Yacht Gondola *provides a trip back in time on Coniston Water*

spectacular being at Hardknott guarding Eskdale. The Celtic communities, deserted by the Romans, suffered invasions by the Angles who settled on the coastal plains where they could use their ox-ploughs, and by the Vikings from the Isle of Man and Ireland who penetrated deep into the valleys to pasture their sheep on the fells. They established the small individual settlements that are still a feature of the lakeland landscape. Norse names predominate everywhere – hills are always fells, streams are becks, and the numerous 'thwaites' are derived from the Norse meaning 'a clearing'.

With the Norman Conquest came castles such as those at Penrith, Brougham and Kendal. Great religious houses endowed with large tracts of land were established, notably at Furness, St Bees and Calder. Influential families, granted land close to the border with the Scots, built their easily-defended peel towers which later often formed the nucleus of a stately home. Border raids and wars led to the building of other peel towers for villagers and their animals, chiefly along the threatened north-east fringe. The Tudors brought more peaceful times, but Henry VIII's dissolution of the monasteries, one of the results of which was extensive unemployment, caused much distress. However, the distribution of monastic lands into lay hands led to the emergence of a new class of yeoman farmers so much admired by Wordsworth. Known as 'estatesmen' (later they were termed 'statesmen'), they held their lands on a fixed-rent basis and were free to manage their estates as they chose. They prospered chiefly on the sale of wool from their hardy Herdwick sheep.

Beautiful Eskdale near the former mining village of Boot

Romantic Watendlath Tarn and village, the setting for Hugh Walpole's Judith Paris

Resourceful and thrifty, they covered the valley floors with a network of fields, patterned the fells with stone-walled enclosures and built the attractive farms on the simple 'statesman plan' that we see today. Basically, this consisted of the 'firehouse', which was the family's living room, and the 'downhouse', the working area, divided by a central hall. Town End in Troutbeck, now the property of the National Trust, is a splendid example.

Looking at the peaceful fells today it is hard to imagine that once they were smoky with industry. The Romans were possibly the first to mine the rich iron seams, and throughout the Middle Ages iron was smelted on hearths beside the lakeshores to be transported by boat and pack-horse train to the coast. Copper and lead were mined in the Newlands valley. The scars of the copper mines on the slopes of the Old Man above Coniston are still prominent, as are the remains of the lead mine at Greenside near Glenridding. Graphite was discovered near Seathwaite in Borrowdale. Known locally as 'wadd', it was in great demand to make casts for coins, round shot and

The great peel tower of Dacre Castle – one of the finest in Cumbria

cannon balls, and later it contributed to the manufacture of the world's first pencils. Slate quarries became important in the eighteenth century, and the lovely green slate from mines above Honister Pass is still worked and valued today. Water-powered mills had always played a vital part in the lives of these isolated communities, and with the growth of the textile industry in the nineteenth century water was put to a new use. A huge demand for bobbins to hold the twine, wire and thread led to the building of many bobbin mills. A restored mill can be seen at Stott Park.

The decline of local industries has been offset by the growth of tourism. A greater appreciation of wild countryside fostered in the early days by the Romantic movement, more leisure time and easier access have been contributory factors. In his *Guide to the Lakes* Wordsworth, wishing to preserve the area's traditional way of life and conserve the landscape, suggested that the Lake District should be considered 'a sort of national property, in which every man has a right and interest who has an eye to perceive and a heart to enjoy'. This principle underlies the work of the National Trust, the National Park Authority and other responsible bodies who ensure the Lake District remains a place of tranquil beauty for us all to enjoy.

ENJOY YOUR TOUR

The tours in this book are designed to cover the Lake District National Park and some of the most attractive surrounding areas which are closely linked to it by historical and economic ties. Towns have been chosen as starting points for ease of access, but as all the tours are circular they can be started at any point on the route.

It is a good plan to read the route directions through before starting a tour as Lake District roads can get busy with impatient users! To make the tours easier to follow the navigational instructions have been printed in bold. There are also boxed letters which tie in with those on the map. Their purpose is to aid your navigation and, in many instances, highlight sections of the route requiring particular attention. The times given for each tour cover motoring only but, if you decide to explore footpaths or visit attractions, they can take the best part of a day. It is possible that opening times for the various attractions may have changed, and it is advisable to telephone before visiting. If you plan more extensive walks the Pathfinder guides, Pathfinder maps or the OS Outdoor Leisure maps at 1: 25 000 (2½ inches to 1 mile/4 cm to 1 km) are ideal. For details see inside back cover.

In order to see some of the loveliest valleys it has been necessary to include limited stretches of narrow roads with passing places. It is always wise to take these very slowly and be prepared to back the car if necessary. You are also likely to come across animals, especially sheep, wandering about on the road – please take care as they have not learned to look both ways! And, finally, be prepared for weather conditions to change suddenly, particularly on the high mountain passes.

LITERARY LANDSCAPE

THE Lake District and William Wordsworth are inseparable. He caught the wild beauty of the lakes and fells in all their moods and, however prosaic his poetry may be at times, it is never lacking in truth and intensity of feeling. After traumatic experiences in France during the Revolution, he turned to nature for healing, helped by the lively observation of his sister Dorothy. Nature became important to him as 'the nurse, the guide, the guardian of my heart, and soul of all my moral being', and he saw man as having his own place in the natural world. Wordsworth is the poet of *Daffodils* and also the poet of *Michael*, the story of a lakeland shepherd battling against adversity.

Born in Cockermouth in 1770, within sight of the lakeland fells, Wordsworth spent happy days at the Grammar School in Hawkshead. Here he 'bounded like a roe among the hills', absorbing almost unconsciously the impressions he was to record later in his poetry. A legacy made it possible for him to devote his time to writing, and in December 1799 he and his sister Dorothy set up home together in Dove Cottage, near Grasmere, to 'live in retirement' among their native mountains.

Dove Cottage is now a place of pilgrimage for many thousands. Dorothy describes their lives and favourite walks together in her Journals, and you can follow in their footsteps around Grasmere, Rydal Water and Ambleside, and take the same path up Easedale to the tarn where they saw the rainbow which inspired the poem. The presence of Wordsworth can be felt everywhere in lakeland, but perhaps even more strongly in wilder places such as the shore of Grisedale Tarn on the slopes of Helvellyn, where he said a final goodbye to his brother John. Tour 2 is a special 'Wordsworth tour'.

William Wordsworth

Attracted by Wordsworth, other nineteenth-century writers came to visit or settle in the Lake District. Coleridge rented Greta Hall overlooking the Derwent, just west of Keswick (now part of a school). Southey came to stay and, after Coleridge's departure, took possession of the house, caring for his own and Coleridge's family until his death in 1843. He is buried in Crosthwaite churchyard. Although not primarily concerned with Lake District scenery, his poetry includes a delightful description of the Lodore Falls.

*The Newlands
valley, the home
of Beatrix Potter's
Mrs Tiggy-Winkle*

De Quincey, author of *The Confessions of an English Opium-Eater*,
married a local girl, Margaret Simpson, and lived happily at Nab
Cottage by Rydal Water. Sir Walter Scott climbed Helvellyn with
Wordsworth and, impressed with the dramatic scenery, set his
romantic *Bridal of Triermain* in St Johns-in-the-Vale.

The Spedding family, who owned Mirehouse beside Bassenthwaite
Lake, invited many eminent literary figures to stay with them.
Among their guests was Tennyson who composed the final stanzas
of *Idylls of the King* on the lakeshore. At the age of 5½ Ruskin
was taken by his nurse to see the view of Derwent Water from Friars
Crag. Today, a plaque records the event. He never forgot the deep
impression made on him by this glimpse of the Lake District, and in
1872 he bought Brantwood on the eastern shore of Coniston Water
where he lived until his death in 1900. He is buried in Coniston
churchyard just across the lake from his home. Memories of
childhood visits to Coniston Water inspired Arthur Ransome to write
Swallows and Amazons, the first of his splendid series of children's
books set in the Lake District. His grave can be visited in Rusland
churchyard overlooking one of the loveliest of all lakeland valleys.

Sir Hugh Walpole is another author commemorated at Keswick.
He settled at Brackenburn beside Derwent Water and used many
Lake District settings for *The Herries Chronicles*. All readers of
Beatrix Potter's delightful tales for children will wish to visit her
cottage, Hill Top, at Near Sawrey. Tour 7 covers the countryside
most closely associated with her.

The Lake District continues to inspire modern writers. These
include Margaret Forster, John Wyatt and Melvyn Bragg. The fine
poetry of Norman Nicholson, centred around Millom in sight
of the western fells, draws its strength from the same source as
Wordsworth, man's place in nature. Wordsworth celebrates the
simple country people, Nicholson the miners, but they both speak
with the same voice.

THE LANGDALES, WAST WATER AND THE DUDDON VALLEY

55 MILES – 2½ HOURS
DURING BUSY PERIODS ALLOW EXTRA TIME FOR THE VERY STEEP ASCENTS OF WRYNOSE AND HARDKNOTT PASSES
START AND FINISH AT AMBLESIDE

The spectacular mountain scenery of the Langdales and the dramatic screes of Wast Water, visited early in this exciting tour, contrast vividly with the return route which follows the wooded, pastoral valley of Wordsworth's beloved Duddon through the Furness fells. Care is needed in negotiating the passes at Wrynose and Hardknott, but the effort is well worthwhile and the views from the top are breathtaking.

From the centre of Ambleside take the A593 (Coniston road). Cross the bridge over the River Rothay and continue along the A593 on its north bank. The road then follows the north bank of the River Brathay to Clappersgate. Pass the junction with the B5286 and continue along the wooded shore of the Brathay for about 1½ miles to approach Skelwith Bridge. Just before the bridge, as the A593 turns left to cross the Brathay **A**, leave the main road and continue along the B5343 for Elterwater. The road bears right beneath Neaum Crag. and the National Trust's Silverthwaite car park can be seen to the right. A delightful walk along the shore of Elter Water leads from the car park. Cross the road and go through a gap in the wall to follow a path through the woods to reach the River Brathay. Bear right to the lakeshore. You can follow the footpath to Elterwater village.

To continue the drive, keep ahead along the B5343. The road climbs to give splendid views of Elter Water backed by the distinctive outline of the Langdale Pikes. **Turn left to Elterwater.** The village is attractively grouped around a small green and has a car park by the lakeside. There is no longer a gunpowder works in the village, but the green slate quarries nearby are still working, supplying both export and home markets. 'Elter Water' is a Norse name and means 'the lake of the swans'. Whooper swans still visit the lake in winter.

Return to the B5343 to approach Chapel Stile at the foot of Great Langdale.

The road runs through this magnificent valley, along the foot of crags that seem to rise almost sheer from the flat plain threaded by Great Langdale Beck and its numerous tributaries. This is Lake District scenery at its finest. **About 1½ miles from Chapel Stile the road crosses the beck near the New Hotel.** There are car parks here. Behind the hotel a short climb leads to a splendid waterfall, Dungeon Ghyll Force.

Continue along the road for another mile to the Old Hotel where the B5343 ends. The old route ahead is now a precipitous green track running up Bow Fell! **So turn left B along the narrow minor road, which climbs steeply, to follow the rim of an upland combe sheltering peaceful Blea Tarn.** There is a car park to the left of the road, just past the tarn, with access to the waterside.

The road descends to a T-junction in Little Langdale. Perhaps this secluded valley is not as grand as its neighbour, but it is surrounded by glorious lakeland fells. **Turn right C past Fell Foot Farm.** A smuggler, Lanty Slee, used to store his contraband here. Immediately after the farm you will see a small terraced hill thought to be a Viking 'Thing Mount' or meeting place.

The road now climbs over Wrynose Pass, drops to Cockley Beck, then climbs again over Hardknott Pass. Near the summit there is a small parking area. Magnificent views of Eskdale open ahead and you can look down on the Roman Fort, 400 feet (122 m) below, built around AD 100 to guard the pass. The outlines of the buildings, which included a granary, a house for the commandant (the men lived in wooden huts) and a bath house, are clearly visible.

The route takes you down towards the Esk valley, Dorothy Wordsworth's 'glittering serpent stream'. Adjacent to the Roman Fort there is a parking area to

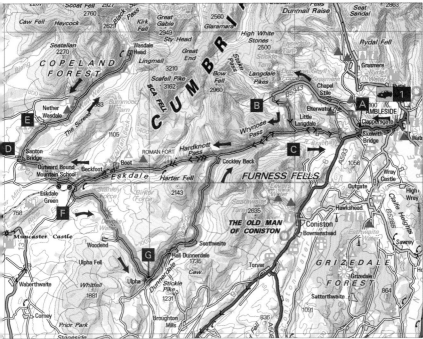

the right of the road. **Follow the road along the valley, making a short detour down a lane on the right to cross a pack-horse bridge, and visit the mill at Boot, if you wish.** Dalegarth Station is just beyond the turning to Boot, offering an opportunity for a steam train ride of 7 miles to Ravenglass on the coast. Riverside walks lead from the station car parks.

Continue along the valley to a T-junction opposite the George IV pub. Turn right, following signs to Holmrook and Whitehaven, and continue through Eskdale Green. Cross the River Mite and ignore a minor road on the left. Continue for Wasdale along the wooded valley at the foot of Irton Pike towards Santon Bridge. The road descends and passes a minor road to Irton. A few yards further, just before the bridge over the River Irt, turn sharp right D for Wast Water. The road runs through attractive wooded countryside to cross the river at Forest Bridge. Just over the bridge bear right E to take

Looking west across Elter Water to the Langdale Pikes

the road for Wasdale Head. A few yards further, at the T-junction, bear right again for Wasdale Head.

Follow the road along the side of Wast Water, famous for the dramatic, almost vertical screes plunging into the water on the opposite shore. Dominating the head of the valley are the dark slopes of Scafell and Great Gable. There are several parking areas beside the road and a large car park near the Wasdale Head Inn. The inn is now a famous rendezvous for walkers and climbers, but the pack-horse bridge close by is a reminder that, in the seventeenth and eighteenth centuries, the inn was a refuge for traders as Wasdale lay on an important pack-horse route to the coast. From the car park, a footpath leads 200 yards (18 m) to the tiny church.

Retrace your route by Wast Water, through Santon Bridge to Eskdale Green. Continue to the point where

The Ravenglass and Eskdale railway

the road turns left down Eskdale (pub on right) and now leave your former route at F and keep on following the sign to Ulpha. Soon there is an opportunity to see a remote tarn, Devoke Water. It lies about ½ mile west of the road. **Continue along the Ulpha road, for about 2 miles, to a black and white signpost on the right which points**

left down a track for Stanley Ghyll. The bridleway opposite, on the right of the road, leads to Devoke Water. There is room to park beside the track.

The road crosses high fells dotted with cotton grass, with views of Scafell and Scafell Pike, and then descends into the Duddon valley. **At a T-junction turn left G to take the road along the beautiful Duddon**

The rocky shores of Wast Water looking towards Great Gable

Ambleside

Situated in the heart of the Lake District at the head of Lake Windermere, on the A591 (the main north-south through-route) this attractive grey-stone town makes an ideal tourist centre. There are many hotels and guesthouses and a wide range of specialist shops catering for most outdoor activities. Lake steamers leave from nearby Waterhead, there is a public launching site, and delightful walks to Stock Ghyll Waterfall and Loughrigg Fell.

South of the town, where the River Brathay flows into Windermere, are the remains of the Roman fort of Galava. Artifacts

from the site are exhibited in the Lake District History Centre in Lake Road. The older part of the town has many interesting buildings and perhaps the strangest is the tiny seventeenth-century Bridge House built over a stream called Stock Ghyll. It is now a National Trust Information Centre. The present parish church, St Mary the Virgin, was designed by Sir Gilbert Scott. Inside, a mural illustrates an ancient rushbearing ceremony which is performed by children on the first Saturday in July. The Wordsworths collected

their mail from the small post office, and there are memorial windows to the poet and his family in the church.

Great Langdale

Awe-inspiring mountain peaks enclose this most dramatic of Lakeland valleys. To the northwest is the familiar outline of the Langdale Pikes, Pike o'Stickle and Harrison Stickle, and enclosing the head of the dale are the steep slopes of Bow Fell. The rows of stone and slate houses at Chapel Stile were built for the workers in the local slate quarries and the gunpowder works at Elterwater. Many of the seventeenth-century farmhouses you will see in the valley have been acquired by the National Trust who ensure they are maintained as working farms.

Eskdale

The lower Esk wanders through woods and rounded hills to reach the sea at the old Roman port of Ravenglass. It is an enchanting valley which can also be enjoyed by steam, on the fifteen-inch gauge Ravenglass and Eskdale railway, or 'La'al Ratty' as it is known locally. The inland terminus is at Dalegarth. In the past, mines in the valley produced iron and copper and, until 1875, the railway carried the iron ore to the coast. Now, with the help of a preservation society, it operates a daily service for tourists from the end of March to the end of October. Telephone: Ravenglass (01229) 717171.

Originally the railway ran to Boot, just to the north of Dalegarth. This interesting village

preserves a corn mill dating from the sixteenth century which was in use until the 1920s. The mill has been restored by Cumbria County Council. Open Easter–September. Closed Mondays. Telephone: Eskdale (019467) 23335.

Wast Water

Reaching a depth of 258 feet (79 m), Wast Water is the deepest lake in Cumbria and the most dramatic. The first climbing association in Great Britain was founded in the tiny 400-year-old Church of St Olaf at Wasdale Head, said to be the smallest church in England. On the second Saturday in October the village hosts the splendid Wasdale Show. Shepherds and their dogs display their skills, and other events include fell races and displays of Lakeland wrestling.

The River Duddon

The river flows for almost 10 miles through beautiful scenery, from its source among the fells above Wrynose Pass to the sea at Duddon Sands. This well-wooded, pastoral valley was Wordsworth's 'longloved Duddon', the subject of a series of sonnets composed at Christmas, 1819. In the final sonnet *After-Thought* he speaks of the Duddon as 'my partner and my guide'.

The river's gentle beauty leads him to reflect:

We Men, who in our morn of
youth defied
The elements, must vanish; –
be it so!
Enough, if something from our
hands have power
To live, and act, and serve the
future hour.

valley to Seathwaite. The church in the village replaced an earlier one which Wordsworth celebrated in one of his Duddon sonnets. The Reverend Robert Walker, who was curate here for sixty-seven years, is referred to in the sonnet as one 'whose good works formed an endless retinue'.

Continue past Dunnerdale Forest where a car park gives

access to forest walks. **The road follows the River Duddon for about 1½ miles to meet your former route at Cockley Beck. Turn right over Wrynose Pass.** As the road descends there are glimpses of Little Langdale Tarn. **Continue towards Little Langdale. Shortly after Fell Foot Farm leave your former route and bear right** C

through Little Langdale valley. Pass Little Langdale Tarn. At the next T-junction turn right for Ambleside. When the road meets the A593 turn left for Skelwith Bridge. Keep to the A593, which bears right after the bridge, and retrace your former route through Clappersgate back to Ambleside. ▪

WORDSWORTH COUNTRY: GRASMERE, RYDAL AND DOCKRAY

40 MILES – 1½ HOURS
ALLOW EXTRA TIME FOR VISITING DOVE COTTAGE AND RYDAL MOUNT
START AND FINISH AT AMBLESIDE

This tour around Helvellyn, in the heart of the Lake District, includes visits to the homes of William and Dorothy Wordsworth, and the beautiful countryside around Grasmere and Rydal Water which inspired so much of their work. More of their favourite haunts are explored as the route follows St John's in the Vale to Dockray and Aira Force near the southern tip of Ullswater. The route returns to Ambleside over Kirkstone Pass. The pass is the highest in the Lake District but presents few difficulties to the motorist. However, snow can fall on the pass as early as October.

Leave Ambleside on the A591 signed to Keswick, heading north for Rydal and Grasmere. On your left rise the tree-covered lower slopes of Loughrigg Fell. **Pass the narrow road on the right for Kirkstone,** aptly named The Struggle, which climbs steeply to the top of Kirkstone Pass. **Keep on as the road dips to cross Rydal Beck and enter the village**. You will catch a glimpse of the impressive eighteenth-century facade of Rydal Hall on the right. Once the home of the le Flemings, an important Lakeland family, it is now owned by the Church of England as a study centre. The Rydal sheep-dog trials are held in the grounds on the second Thursday after the first Monday in August. The house is not open to the public.

Wordsworth moved to nearby Rydal Mount in 1813 and lived there until his death in 1850. His former home is open to visitors.

To visit the house, turn right off the A591 up the steep lane signposted to Rydal Mount. The house contains fine family portraits, many of the poet's personal possessions, furniture, and first editions of his works. Continue down the lane to visit the church where Wordsworth worshipped, and the field close by which the poet planted with daffodils to please his daughter Dora.

Return to the A591. This

Brothers Water from Kirkstone Pass

road now follows the northern shore of Rydal Water, a beautiful little lake surrounded by mixed woodlands and bordered to the south and north by the steep slopes of Loughrigg Fell and Rydal Fell. In about ½ mile you will see a white house standing alone to the right of the road. This is Nab Cottage, once the home of Thomas De Quincey, friend of the Wordsworths and author of *The Confessions of an English Opium-Eater.*

The road leaves the lakeshore to climb White Moss, a steep promontory threaded by the River Rothay, separating Grasmere from Rydal Water. For a wonderful view of Grasmere and a walk in Wordsworth's footsteps, stop at the car park on White Moss Common. Follow the short circular walk over White Moss which takes you to Dove Cottage and returns through the woods and beside the River Rothay.

Follow the A591 as it fringes the eastern shore of Grasmere. There is a splendid view of Grasmere vale dominated by Helm Crag, which is topped by the curious rock formations known as The Lion and The Lamb. **In Town End turn right along the old pack-horse road** signposted to Dove Cottage to visit the Wordsworths' home. This is a simple whitewashed building which was originally an inn called the Dove and Olive Branch. It has a tiny porch where Dorothy would often chat to weary travellers. At that time the low windows of the living room overlooked the lake. Wordsworth often composed his poems on the seat in the hillside garden.

Return to the A591 and take the first road on the left to visit Grasmere village. At busy times leave your car in the car park to the right of the road as you approach Grasmere village and explore on foot. **Return to your car and drive through the village. The road bears right to rejoin the A591 in front of the Swan Inn.** This inn was the subject of one of Wordsworth's poems. **Turn left to follow the A591 as it climbs Dunmail Raise.** This was the appropriately gloomy setting for a battle in AD943 between the Norse King Dunmail of Cumbria and the Anglo-Saxon King Edmund of Northumbria who was the victor. It is still a lonely and desolate place. On the right a little lane leads to Michael's Nook, the site of the sheepfold which the old shepherd Michael attempted to

Aira Force

build in the absence of his son. Wordsworth's fine poem *Michael* tells his story.

The road runs across the bleak watershed of Dunmail Raise for almost 5 miles before descending to follow the eastern shore of Thirlmere. Wythburn church is all that remains of the submerged village that once stood at the southern end of the valley. There is a car park close to the church about ½ mile down the lakeside. Two miles further along the shore there are more car parks. A short circular forest trail with fine views begins from Swirls car park to the right of the road. The other car park a little further on the left, Station Coppice, gives access to the waterside.

Continue past Thirlspot Inn and, in a little over 4 miles, at the north end of the reservoir, the B5322 signposted to Threlkeld meets the A591 on the right **A**. Leave the A591 and continue along the B5322 for about ¼ mile. A narrow road on the left, just before some large sheds, leads to Legburthwaite car park. (There is a very discreet sign.) This is a lovely place for a picnic. Turn left into the car park. Walk through two small wooden gates over a lane to the

---

• PLACES OF INTEREST •

Rydal Mount
The house is open March–October daily 9.30–5. November–February Wednesday–Monday 10–6. Telephone: Ambleside (015394) 33002.

Grasmere
Dove Cottage at Town End, near Grasmere village, was William and Dorothy Wordsworth's first home. They arrived together in 1799 and stayed until 1808. During that time Wordsworth wrote some of his finest poetry, inspired by the lakeland scenery and its people. For him, Grasmere was 'the loveliest spot that man hath ever found'. He acknowledged his debt to Dorothy, saying 'she gave me eyes, she gave me ears'. Her *Grasmere Journal* records in prose many scenes he afterwards described in verse. The cottage is open daily 9.30–5.30. Closed 10 January–6 February. Telephone: Grasmere (015394) 35544 or 35547. The Grasmere and Wordsworth Museum is opposite the cottage.

Grasmere is a beautiful, circular, glacial lake with a single central island sheltered to the north by the great mountain range of Helvellyn.

St Oswald's Church in the village is well-known for its rush-bearing ceremony held on the Saturday nearest 5 August, and in the churchyard you will find the Wordsworth family graves. By the entrance gate is the tiny former schoolroom which is now the famous gingerbread shop. The secret recipe is so valuable it has to be kept in the vaults of the local bank! Grasmere Sports are held on the nearest Thursday to the 20 August.

Thirlmere
In 1879 the Manchester Corporation joined and expanded two small lakes, Leathe's Water and Wythburn Water, to form this reservoir, drowning 463 acres of farmland in the process. Wythburn church was a favourite meeting place for both Wordsworth and Coleridge.

Aira Force
This spectacular waterfall, described by Wordsworth as 'the powerful brook which dashes amongst rocks through a deep glen', is one of the most beautiful in the Lake District. It has a fall of 60 feet (18 m) and a succession of paths and bridges provide excellent viewpoints.

Nearby is Gowbarrow Park where Dorothy Wordsworth saw, and described in her diary, the lakeside daffodils that William was later to immortalise in his famous poem.

Glenridding
Once a mining village, Glenridding, ideally situated on the southern shores of Ullswater, is now a tourist centre. The remains of Greenside lead mines, closed in 1962, can be seen on the common above the village.

Two steamers, *Lady of the Lake* and *Raven* operate a daily scheduled service in the season from the pier. Telephone: Glenridding (017684) 82229.

It is possible to cross the lake to Howtown situated on the quiet

eastern shore, or travel north the full 7 miles of Ullswater to Pooley Bridge.

Patterdale
The name of this small village is derived from 'St Patrick's Dale'. There is a legend that St Patrick, shipwrecked on Duddon Sands, visited the dale. He gave his name to the church in its lovely setting, framed by the mountains of the Helvellyn and High Street ranges.

Sheep-dog trials are held here on the late summer Bank Holiday Saturday.

Hartsop and Brothers Water
Hartsop – the valley of the deer – is a fascinating little village. It has retained some seventeenth-century farm buildings and, attached to some of the houses, are the open-fronted spinning galleries so vital to cottage economy in the past.

Tiny Brothers Water, only ½ mile long and ¼ mile wide, is named after two brothers who are said to have drowned in the lake. Wordsworth records that it was 'While resting on the bridge at the foot of Brothers Water' that he began his poem *Written in March*.

picnic tables beautifully sited in the meadows beside St John's Beck. Readers of the novels of Walter Scott will recognise the Castle Rock of Triermain close by.

The road runs north through the charming pastoral valley of St John's in the Vale. This comes as a sharp contrast after the darkly-wooded shores of Thirlmere. The valley is said to take its name from the Knights Hospitallers of St John who may have founded a church here. **The road follows the valley for over 4 miles to meet the A66 Keswick-Penrith road B. Turn right along the A66.** The great mass of Skiddaw and Blencathra is on your left and Helvellyn on your right. **Continue for 5 miles, ignoring all side roads, to the junction with the A5091 on the right C. Turn right to drive south down Matterdale. Drive through the hamlet of Matterdale End.** About 1 mile further, look for Matterdale church beside a minor road signposted to Penruddock. There is a parking area by the church gate. This is a perfect example of a solidly-built Lakeland church, completed in 1573 by the Pattinson family who have been building in the Lake District for over four hundred years. From the seat outside there is a marvellous view across the valley to Place Fell and High Street.

Drive through Dockray for Ullswater. There are glorious views of the lake as the road descends the fell to the northern shore. **Here the A5091 meets the A592 D. To see Aira Force, turn left along the A592 for a few yards.** Follow the footpath from the car park. The Wordsworths often walked this way and Dorothy records in her *Grasmere Journal* several visits to nearby Gowbarrow Park.

Retrace your route past the junction with the A5091 and continue along the A592 which hugs the shore of Ullswater. Continue through Glenridding. Just past the bridge to the right of the road, opposite the Ullswater Boat Stores, is moss-hung St Patrick's Well.

The road leaves Ullswater behind to cross Grisedale Bridge and climb the fells beside the Goldrill Beck. Continue through Patterdale village and keep to the main road as it crosses the Deepdale Beck at Bridgend.

In a little over 1 mile turn left along a little road signposted to Hartsop E. This fascinating Lakeland village, with its old houses, must not be missed! Drive through the village to a large car park to explore on foot.

Drive back to the A592 to continue beside Brothers Water and cross Kirkstone Pass. Opposite the Kirkstone Pass Inn, built in 1496, you pass the old road, The Struggle, which leads down to Ambleside on the right. In the past, coach passengers wisely alighted and walked down to the village, and today, unwary cyclists can some-times be seen trying to straighten bent wheels and handlebars at the foot of the hill! **Continue down the A592, past the church at Troutbeck, to meet the A591 which runs along the eastern shore of Windermere. Turn right along the A591 to return to Ambleside and complete the tour.** ■

Dove Cottage

TARN HOWS, CONISTON WATER AND ULVERSTON

46 MILES - 2 HOURS
START AND FINISH AT CONISTON

From the magnificent viewpoint of Tarn Hows, this tour follows the eastern shore of Coniston Water to explore the Furness fells and visit the historic towns of Ulverston and Dalton-in-Furness. A highlight of this route is a visit to the extensive ruins of Furness Abbey. The return route gives splendid views over the Duddon estuary before following the western shore of Coniston Water back to Coniston.

This charming memorial, recalling Queen Victoria's Diamond Jubilee in 1897, stands in Dalton market place

Leave Coniston on the B5285 heading east for Hawkshead. The road crosses Yewdale Beck and runs through Waterhead to the lakeside at Kirby Quay. Continue along the road as it curves round the top of the lake and then bears left signposted to Hawkshead, Windermere and Tarn Hows. Go past the exit road from Tarn Hows – a one-way system operates here – and follow the road uphill to take the road on the left signposted to Ambleside by Barngates. After about ¹⁄₄ mile take the next road on the left signed to Tarn Hows. A narrow road with passing places winds through woods to the tarn. It is a good idea to leave your car in one of the car parks and walk down to the waterside.

Continue straight on through a valley bordered by ferns along the exit road which brings you back to the B5285. Turn right to retrace your route to the head of Coniston Water. Leave the B5285 and turn left , to follow the beautiful lakeside road along the eastern shore. You pass Tent Lodge on the right, where Alfred Tennyson spent an idyllic honeymoon, driving, walking and boating. A little further down the road is Low Bank Farm, Arthur Ransome's 'Holly Howe', the setting for his well-loved book *Swallows and Amazons*. The road runs closer to the shore to bring you to John Ruskin's house, Brantwood, which is open to visitors. Across the lake is a fine view of Coniston Hall, a magnificent fifteenth-century manor, recognisable by

Picturesque Tarn Hows, a popular picnic spot

its tall cylindrical chimneys. Sir Richard le Fleming built the first manor on this site in 1250. The cruck-built hall where he housed his servants, huntsmen and bowmen still stands at Bowmanstead, close by.

Continue along the lakeshore through oak and beech woods with several car parks and picnic places. You pass two small islands where landing is permitted, Fir Island and Peel Island. All readers of *Swallows and Amazons* will recognise the latter as 'Wild Cat Island'.

Shortly after, the road runs through High Nibthwaite where Arthur Ransome spent his childhood holidays. Until the coming of the railway this quiet spot bustled with life. The smelted iron and copper, brought by boat from Kirby Quay near Coniston village, was unloaded here and taken by waggon and pack-horse to Ulverston.

The road now follows the east bank of the River Crake. A row of wind generators runs along the top of the fell on the right. Continue through Low Nibthwaite for about 1 mile then, at the T-junction, turn right B to cross the river at Lowick Bridge. Turn immediately left along the A5084 for Lowick Green, and continue to meet the A5092. Turn right and, after 1/4 mile, turn left just after the first crossroad sign down an unsignposteded minor road. This narrow, gated road runs along the fellside above Otley Beck giving views of another Lakeland, untouched by the twentieth century. **The road drops into the valley just south of the village of Broughton Beck to meet the B5281. Turn left C along the B5281.**

Keep to the B5281 as it bears right and enters Ulverston. Turn left following the one-way system to a large roundabout. Bear right along the A590 signed for Barrow.

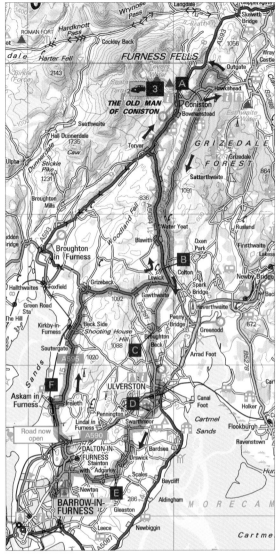

Go straight over the first set of traffic lights then turn left into Princes Road signed to the Station and Swarthmoor Hall. Cross the railway and continue to the next Swarthmoor Hall sign. Turn right following the sign into Urswick Road. After about 1/4 mile take the minor road on the right D which soon turns sharp left. Now you have a view of Swarthmoor Hall. Dating from the seventeenth century, the hall is an important centre for the Quaker movement. It was the home of Margaret Fell who, after the death of her first husband, married George Fox the founder of the Society of Friends. The house is still owned by the Society and is open to the public.

Retrace your route to the Urswick road and turn right following the sign for Urswick. Continue for a little under 1 mile to a T-junction. Turn right and continue for 1/2 mile to the crossroads just past High Carley, and turn left for Great Urswick. The houses of the village are clustered around a tarn. **Drive through the village, the tarn is on your**

John Ruskin's former home, Brantwood, overlooking Coniston Water

left, to the Church of St Mary. A rush-bearing ceremony is still performed here. Inside, there is much of interest including box pews, a rare three-decker pulpit and part of a ninth-century Anglo-Saxon cross.

Continue to drive through Little Urswick. Pass the Swan Inn and, as the road turns left, turn right to follow a minor road to a T-junction. Turn right **E** for Dalton-in-Furness. Drive through Stainton with Adgarley and go straight over the first crossroads. In 3/4 mile turn left following the sign for Newton. In just under 1/2 mile the road forks. Take the right-hand road which drops steeply downhill to the valley of the Mill Beck. At the foot the road forks again. Follow the right-hand road as it crosses the railway and curves round the red sandstone ruins of Furness Abbey framed by the thickly-wooded slopes of the Vale of Nightshade. The abbey is open to visitors. A car park is on the left but, if you drive a little further, bearing right as the road forks, there is another car park close to the abbey entrance.

Continue past the abbey entrance to meet the main road. Turn right to a traffic island. Ignore the sign on the left and keep straight on over the railway for Dalton. The

The red sandstone ruins of Furness Abbey are a reminder of its former greatness

Coniston

Although this grey slate village on the north-west shore of Coniston Water is now a favourite holiday destination, it still retains the atmosphere of a place that has worked hard for its living. Since Roman times copper has been mined nearby. The remains of the nineteenth-century mines can be seen on the slopes of its sheltering fells which rise to a height of 2,635 feet (803 m), the summit of the Old Man of Coniston. This can be reached on foot and there is a footpath following the western shore of the lake from Coniston to Blawith at its southern tip.

Famous people connected with Coniston include John Ruskin and Malcolm and Donald Campbell. They are commemorated in exhibits in the Ruskin Museum, opened in the village in 1901. A seat has been placed on the village green in memory of Donald Campbell who lost his life on Coniston Water in 1967.

In summer the luxurious steam yacht *Gondola*, first launched in 1859, is based at Coniston Pier and provides regular scheduled trips to Parkamoor on the south-east shore of the lake. For information and bookings telephone: Coniston (015394) 41288.

Also on the pier is the Coniston Boating Centre where sailing, motor and rowing boats can be hired and private boats launched.

Tarn Hows

Three small tarns were converted into this small lake by the Victorian owners of the Monk Coniston Estate. But, although artificial, the result is outstandingly beautiful. You can walk all round the wooded shores of the tarn. From the slopes above there are magnificent views of Coniston Water and mountains, which include Red Screes, Wetherlam , the Helvellyn range and the Langdale Pikes.

Brantwood

John Ruskin, whose views on art, poetry and social issues had such a profound effect on his contemporaries, bought Brantwood without actually seeing it in 1872, believing that 'any place opposite Coniston Old Man must be beautiful'.

He discovered what he called 'a mere shed of rotten timber and loose stone' but, impressed with the splendid view of the lake, he began extensive repairs and alterations to the existing buildings. This work included the addition of a six-sided turret to his bedroom.

The house contains many of Ruskin's paintings and possessions. There is also an exhibition of Alfred Wainwright's original drawings for his illustrated guides to the Lakes.

The nature trail in the grounds leads to Ruskin's stone seat overlooking a waterfall. The house is now owned by the Brantwood Trust. Open daily mid-March to mid-November 11–5.30. Rest of the year Wednesday–Sunday 11–4. Telephone: Coniston (015394) 41396.

Ulverston

Ulverston dates back to Saxon times and was mentioned in the *Domesday Book*. Today, it is an attractive town with fine eighteenth-century houses and a lively street market on Thursdays and Saturdays. Visitors are welcome at the Furness Gallery, where dolls' houses and furniture are made, and the Cumbria Crystal's factory in the old Cattle Market. Stan Laurel was born in Ulverston and 'the world's largest collection of Laurel and Hardy memorabilia' is exhibited in the Laurel and Hardy Museum in Upper Brook Street.

Furness Abbey

Founded in 1123 by Stephen, later King of England, the abbey became one of the wealthiest religious houses in England. The abbot ruled the whole of Furness until the Dissolution. Many fine features survive, including the Norman arches of the cloisters and the canopied seats in the presbytery. Open 1 April–30 September daily 10–6. Rest of year Tuesday–Sunday 10–4. Telephone: Barrow (01229) 23420.

---

road crosses the railway again, and then runs beside Poaka Beck to the centre of this historic little town, once the capital of Furness. At the T-junction turn left to the market-place. This is dominated by the impressive keep of the castle. The keep was used as a court-house by the monks of Furness Abbey. Continue to join the A595 as it bears right to follow the coast north to Askam in Furness. There are superb panoramic views over the sands of the Duddon estuary to the Lake District mountains.

The A595 runs close to the railway in Askam in Furness and then turns sharply right signposted to Broughton **F** . Keep to the A595 as it bears left for Broughton just past the post office along Tippins Lane, heading for Kirkby-in-Furness. The road traces the steep fellside then drops to run close to the marshes inland from the Duddon estuary for 4¹/₂ miles to Grizebeck. This is an attractive village sheltered by green hills. Turn right just past the village along the A5092 for Kendal.

Follow this road across the Furness fells, ignore the turning for Ulverston, and keep on through Gawthwaite to meet the A5084 just south of Lowick Green. Turn left for Coniston to follow the west bank of the River Crake in the direction of Water Yeat at the foot of Coniston Water. Continue along the west shore of the lake. At Oxen House Bay the road bears inland beside Torver Beck to meet the A593 at Torver. Turn right to take this road back to Coniston. ■

CONISTON OLD MAN, THE ULPHA FELLS AND ESKDALE

40 MILES –2 HOURS
START AND FINISH AT CONISTON
DURING BUSY PERIODS ALLOW EXTRA TIME
FOR THE VERY STEEP ASCENT OF HARDKNOTT PASS

A wide variety of contrasting scenery can be enjoyed on this tour. From the towering slopes of the Old Man of Coniston, the route visits the historic village of Broughton in Furness before giving wide views over the sands of the Duddon estuary. The little church by the River Duddon, Wordsworth's 'Kirk of Ulpha', is visited before the tour crosses the lonely Ulpha fells past Devoke Water on the way to Eskdale. The route climbs to the summit of Hardknott Pass to present a panorama of Lakeland's highest mountains and a bird's-eye-view of a Roman fort before returning to Coniston along the lovely Duddon valley.

From the centre of Coniston follow the A593 heading south-west for Broughton in Furness. On the left fields slope down to Coniston Water and, on the right rise the great crags of the Coniston fells dominated by the 2,635-foot (803 m) peak of the Old Man of Coniston. **After about ¹/₂ mile the road runs through Bowmanstead.** The name means 'the dwelling of the bowmen', and it is here you can see the oldest building in Coniston. This is the cruck-built hall constructed in the thirteenth century by Sir Richard le Fleming to house his archers. Coppiced woodlands shade the route as it crosses Torver Beck, one of several mountain streams that feed the lake after rising high in the western fells. After passing Torver village the road runs close to the dismantled Furness railway, built in 1859 to carry minerals from Coniston to the coast.

Coniston Water is concealed by fells as the road takes a more westerly course for another 5 miles to descend to Broughton in Furness, an old market village sheltered by hills, on the north bank of the mouth of the River Duddon. As the road descends there are views over the wide sands of the estuary.

Just before Broughton in Furness the road divides. Keep to the A593, along the left-hand road, to drive to the market square in the centre of this attractive eighteenth-century village. **Facing the square, keep straight ahead for a few yards along the A595. Turn right for Workington, then right again still following the A595. At the T-junction bear left** A **along the A595 as it climbs**

The Duddon valley

26

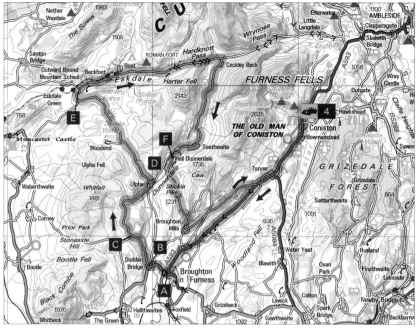

to High Cross. Continue for
Workington. The road runs
downhill to cross the River Lickle,
just before it meets the River
Duddon, then crosses the valley
to approach Duddon Bridge.

Ignore a joining road
on the right which follows
the east bank of the River
Duddon and drive over
Duddon Bridge. The road
bears right for a few yards
then sharply left. Leave the
A595 on the corner **B** and
keep straight on along the
minor road signposted to
Corney which follows the
west bank of the River
Duddon. The road runs through
woods along the Dunnerdale
valley with the river close on the
right. Many small tree-covered
hills are dotted either side of the
river which carves a deep channel
between the rocks. Wordsworth
considered this valley to be the
most beautiful in the Lake District,
and wrote thirty-five sonnets in
praise of his 'majestic Duddon'.

From the bridge the road
follows the riverside for a
little over 1 mile then bears
left and becomes unfenced.
After crossing a cattle-grid

take the minor road on the
right **C** which winds over
the fells to descend into the
Duddon valley at Ulpha.

The road is unfenced
at first until it descends to
cross Logan Beck bridge at
Beckstones. Now it becomes
fenced and leads over lonely
moorland broken by rocky
outcrops. Ignore all joining
roads and follow the way to
Ulpha as it bears right to drop
steeply down Millbrow and

crosses Tongue Beck.
Continue to a T-junction and
bear left following the sign
for Eskdale. (The road on the
right leads over Ulpha Bridge.)
A few yards further the road
bends left. On the corner, close
to the river, stands the famous
'Kirk of Ulpha' celebrated by
Wordsworth in one of his Duddon
sonnets. After the left turn the
road bends right for a few
yards and, when a minor road
continues ahead along the

• *PLACES OF INTEREST* •

Broughton in Furness
This interesting village was
recorded in 1196 as 'Brocton',
the 'settlement by the brook'.
In August its historic charter
is proclaimed in the market
square where you can see the
old stocks, stone-slab stalls and
a clock dated 1766.

The Broughton family settled
in the area in Anglo-Saxon times
and they remained powerful
throughout the Middle Ages. They
built a castle just to the north of
the village. The tower and the
dungeons remain (theses are not

open to the public) and several
public footpaths can be followed
the short distance from the village
to explore the castle grounds.

The Old Town Hall houses
the Jack Hadwin motorcycle
collection. This is a fascinating
assembly of local veteran and
vintage machines; the oldest is
dated 1899 and most are pre-
1937. The exhibition was opened
as the Lakeland Motorcycle
Museum in 1981. Open 1 April–
end October Sunday–Friday
10.30–5. Telephone: Flookburgh
(015395) 58509.

valley, turn left still following the same road as before, for Eskdale . The road climbs steeply through the beautiful woods fringing Crosby Gill. The road continues climbing to cross high fells with magnificent views over the Scafell range. **Continue in the direction for Eskdale Green.**

After about 4 miles look for a black and white signpost on the left pointing right to a track for

A typical Lake District moorland road crossing the high fells to Beckstones

Stanley Ghyll. A bridleway on the left, just past the signpost, leads to remote Devoke Water. It is an easy walk of under 1/2 mile. There is room to park beside the track to Stanley Ghyll.

Return to the road and keep on as it begins a winding descent into Eskdale. Ignore a minor road on the left and follow the road as it curves right to cross the Esk and continues to a T-junction **. Turn right to follow the valley.** There are splendid views of the Scafell range ahead. At Dalegarth it is possible to take a ride to the coast at Ravenglass on the fifteen-inch Ravenglass and Eskdale railway, or 'La'al Ratty' as it is known locally. North of Dalegarth Station a road runs the short distance to the old mining village of Boot where a restored corn mill dating from the sixteenth century is open to the public. The gentle countryside of rounded hills soon gives way to steep crags. **The road leaves the valley of the Esk and begins the steep ascent of Hardknott. Care is needed as the road**

climbs to a height of 1,291 feet (394 m), with gradients of 1-in-3 in some places and some tricky hairpin bends. On the summit a small parking area affords an opportunity to pause and enjoy the magnificent view west over Eskdale. You can also look down on the well-preserved remains of Hardknott Castle, a Roman fort dating from the second century AD.

Continue down the pass, where care is also needed, to descend to Cockley Beck. Turn right here beside the River Duddon once more. A beautiful road leads beside the river. After a little over 1 mile it passes the Dunnerdale Forest where there are several car parks with forest walks. The most delightful is at Froth Pot. A favourite walk from here leads over the bridge and along the path heading south to Birks Bridge, on a famous pack-horse route.

Follow the road as it winds down the valley through Seathwaite. About 1 mile past Seathwaite, just before Hall Bridge, the road divides

Ulpha

This small cluster of houses beside the River Duddon derives its name from Ulf who owned the manor in the eleventh century. The simple Church of St John the Baptist which stands alone above the river – surrounded as Wordsworth wrote by its 'wave-washed churchyard' – inspired one of his finest sonnets. Inside there is much of interest . The altar is made from a single fruit tree and the church retains an original pitch-pipe which was used to help singers find the right note before the installation of an organ.

The Ravenglass and Eskdale Railway

A daily service operates for tourists from the end of March to the end of October. Telephone: Ravenglass (01229) 717171.

Hardknott Castle

The Romans arrived in the Lake District in the first century AD and built a road, a little south of the present route, from Ravenglass on the coast to Ambleside, then along the mountain ridge where it was known as High Street, to Penrith. North of the road they built a fort, Mediobogdum, now known as Hardknott Castle, to command the mountain pass leading to Eskdale and the sea. The fort extends over two acres. It forms a square with ramparts 20 feet (6 m) thick in places. Towers protected each corner and roads crossed to a gate in the middle of each wall. From the summit of the pass the outline of the headquarters building, the granary and the commandant's house can be seen clearly, and there is a parking area beside the road close to the fort. The bath house, fed by a brook, was complete with underfloor heating and a sauna. Ground was levelled to provide a parade ground covering three acres. This wild, exposed fort cannot have been a popular posting with the Balkan troops who manned it!

Seathwaite Church

Built in 1874 the present church replaces an earlier one which was the subject of one of Wordsworth's Duddon sonnets. A memorial in the church commemorates Reverend Robert Walker (1709–1802) who was curate here for sixty-seven years and praised for his good works by Wordsworth. He earned the title of 'Wonderful Walker'. Eminently practical, he made his own furniture, and you can see one of his chairs in the church.

F. **Do not cross the bridge, but continue straight ahead along the left-hand road. This climbs out of the Duddon valley and bears left over the craggy Dunnerdale fells to cross the River Lickle into Broughton Mills.**

As you enter the village look carefully for a turning on the left. The road follows the south bank of the river. **Continue straight over the next crossroads.** There is open moorland on your right, but a large pine forest fringes the road on your left. There are tree-shaded car parks and picnic areas with walks down to the riverside. **This quiet road leaves the forest and, as Hummer Lane, drops steeply down to meet the A593. Turn left to follow this road back to Coniston.** ■

Lakeland's highest peaks from the Ulpha fells

MUNCASTER CASTLE, RAVENGLASS AND BLACK COMBE

50 MILES – 3 HOURS
START AND FINISH AT CONISTON
DURING BUSY PERIODS ALLOW EXTRA TIME FOR THE VERY STEEP ASCENTS OF WRYNOSE AND HARDKNOTT PASSES

This splendid tour follows in the footsteps of the Roman legions to their major port on the north-west coast at Ravenglass where the remains of their Bath House are some of the best-preserved ruins in the country. A visit to Muncaster Castle is followed by a coastal drive which turns inland round the base of Black Combe, said to be one of the oldest mountains in the world. The return route follows the west shore of Coniston Water.

Leave Coniston village heading north-east along the A593 for Ambleside. After passing a minor road on the right the road runs beside a stream along the Yewdale valley dominated by the steep crags of the Yewdale fells. **After crossing Glen Mary Bridge the heading becomes more northerly as the road hugs the shore of Yew Tree Tarn and continues in the direction of Skelwith Bridge. Do not go as far as the bridge but, in a little over 1 mile past the tarn, turn left along the minor road signposted to Wrynose, Elterwater and the Langdales A** . The road descends for a few yards then enters the trees of Tongue Intake Plantation owned by the National Trust.

The road divides at the approach to Little Langdale B . **Take the left-hand road to follow the River Brathay into this beautiful valley.** The Romans came this way, along their road from Waterhead near Ambleside to Ravenglass on the west coast, and the tour now traces their route. **Continue past the hotel and post office.**

• PLACES OF INTEREST •

The Ravenglass and Eskdale Railway
A daily service operates for tourists from the end of March to the end of October. Telephone: Ravenglass (01229) 717171.

Muncaster Mill
This working water-powered corn mill dates from about 1700. Visitors can see the early Victorian machinery producing stone-ground flours and oatmeals which are on sale. The mill is open April–May, September–October daily 11–5. June–August daily 10.30–5.30. Telephone: Ravenglass (01229) 717232.

Muncaster Castle
The oldest part of the castle dates from the thirteenth century when it became the home of the Pennington family. The building is flanked by two towers, one of which is a defensive peel tower built on Roman foundations in 1325. The castle was enlarged in the fifteenth and sixteenth centuries.

Fine family portraits and an outstanding collection of sixteenth- and seventeenth-century furniture can be seen here.

The 'Luck of Muncaster' is a fragile glass bowl, decorated with gold and enamel. This was presented to the family by a grateful Henry VI. After his defeat at the battle of Hexham in 1464 he was found wandering on Muncaster Fell by a shepherd who took him to the castle. It is said that as long as the bowl remains

intact the succession of the family is ensured.

The grounds are open all year 11–5, and the castle from Easter to end October 1–4.30. Closed on Mondays. Telephone: Ravenglass (01229) 717614/717203.

Ravenglass
The village is situated where the rivers which thread Wasdale, Miterdale and Eskdale flow into the sea and it was once a busy port. A woodland walk of less than 1/2 mile leads from the station to the site of the Roman fort, Glannoventa, built in AD78. It was linked to the inland fort at Waterhead by the Tenth Highway. The bath house, known as Walls Castle, built of red sandstone, still has walls 12 feet (3.5 m) high.

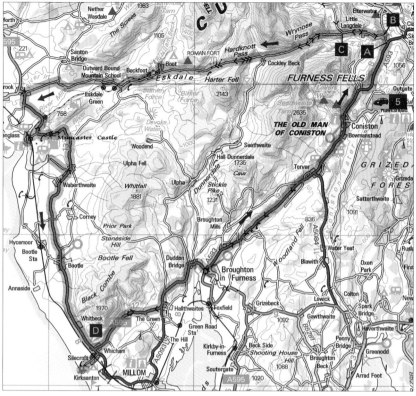

The road climbs a little above the north bank of Little Langdale Tarn which is ringed by stone-walled, green fields at the foot of some of Lakeland's most magnificent mountains: Crinkle Crags and Pike O'Blisco to the north and to the south the Tilberthwaite fells rising to the Wetherlam. **Past the tarn the road divides C. Take the left-hand road to follow the valley past Fell Foot Farm.** This is one of several farms in the valley owned by the National Trust. In the past, when smuggling was a profitable occupation, the most notorious free trader was Lanty Slee who stored his illicit goods in a room at Fell Foot. Near the farm is a green terraced mound which is possibly a Viking 'Thing Mount' or meeting place.

The valley is left behind as the road climbs the bleak slope of Wrynose Pass. At the summit (1,281 feet/390 m) you will see the tall Three Shires Stone on the right of the road. Before the whole Lakeland area was designated as Cumbria, the stone marked the point where the boundaries of Lancashire, Westmorland and Cumberland met. **A steep descent leads down to Cockley Beck where a joining road runs south down Dunnerdale. Ignore this road and continue up the very** **steep ascent of Hardknott Pass which needs taking carefully as the gradient is 1-in-3 in places with tricky hairpin bends.** Pause in the parking place on the summit to enjoy a wonderful view west down Eskdale. The Roman legions will have seen the same view from their fort, the outlines of which

The Ravenglass and Eskdale Railway

31

Waberthwaite

This small village has gained an international reputation for the quality of its Cumberland sausages. These are made in a continuous strip from pork flavoured with herbs. You should accompany your sausages with a sauce made from Bramley apples, brown sugar and a little mace.

Bootle

The *Domesday Book* records a settlement here beside the River Annas within easy reach of the sea. Two lanes lead to the coast, one to Annaside at the mouth of the river, and the other to a pleasant beach at Tarn Bay.

The Church of St Michael was built by the Normans, and traces of their work can be seen in the chancel. There is an interesting memorial to Sir Hugh Agnew who was Henry VIII's cellarer.

He acquired the site of the nearby Benedictine nunnery after the dissolution of the monasteries.

East of the village, on the northern slopes of Black Combe, Bronze Age settlements have been found. Over 10,000 cairns dot the fells and near Swinside stands the remarkable Sunkenkirk Stone Circle.

Black Combe

This lonely peak in the south-west corner of the Lake District National Park has, for hundreds of years, proved to be a valuable landmark for sailors.

The base of the mountain covers a very wide area. The view from the summit is one of the finest in Britain. Inland lie the peaks of Lakeland and to the west it is possible to see the Isle of Man and mountains in Wales, Scotland and Ireland.

steam and diesel engines. Opened originally in 1882 to carry iron the 7 miles from the Nab Gill mines at Boot to the coast, this little railway provides a restful way to enjoy views of the valley of the River Mite. A $1/2$-mile walk from the station crosses the Esk to Gill Force waterfall and another $1/2$ mile takes you to Stanley Ghyll Force, a dramatic sequence of falls in a tree-lined gorge.

The rugged surroundings give way to fields and rounded hills as you continue down the valley. **At the T-junction turn right for Holmrook and Ravenglass. Cross the railway.** The road curves left past a pleasant wood where there is a car park with access to forest walks. **Cross the River Mite and, a little further on, turn left down a minor road signposted to Holmrook, Ravenglass, Gosforth and Whitehaven. This runs to a T-junction. Turn left, following the sign for Holmrook, along a straight road leading to the A595. Turn left for Ravenglass. Keep to the A595 as it crosses the River Mite by Muncaster Mill.** The mill is open for visitors and is one of the stopping places for the Ravenglass and Eskdale railway.

Leave the main road as it turns left, and turn right

you can see on a shelf of the fell 400 feet (122 m) below. For a closer look you can walk to the fort from a parking area to the right of the road on the descent.

Follow the road as it descends into Eskdale and continues along the valley. Turn right to make an interesting detour to Boot. This is a small village nestling

beneath the fells. A pack-horse bridge over the Whillan Beck leads to the restored sixteenth-century corn mill, open from Easter to September.

Return to the Eskdale road and continue a little further down the valley to Dalegarth. This is the inland terminus for the fifteen-inch gauge Ravenglass and Eskdale railway, which uses both

The quiet village of Ravenglass, once a busy port, at the confluence of the Irt and the Esk

The rounded outline of Black Combe, an isolated outcrop of Skiddaw slate

to follow a minor road and reach the coast at the old Roman port of Ravenglass. This is now an attractive village facing the wide dunes at the mouth of the River Esk. The estuary is a nature reserve. As you approach the village, just after the first railway bridge, you will see the car park for the Ravenglass and Eskdale railway on the left. Adjacent is the Ravenglass Railway Museum. Information about the area's wildlife can be obtained from the tourist information centre in the car park .

Retrace the route to join the A595. Leave the former route here and keep straight on along the A595 following the signs for Barrow. After about 1/2 mile you will see a sign for Muncaster Castle and a large car park on the left of the road opposite the entrance. This magnificent building and its beautiful grounds are open to the public. There are splendid views from here of Eskdale and the mountains beyond.

Continue the tour along

the A595 for Waberthwaite and Bootle. To see a little of Lakeland of long ago take a turning on the right for Hall Waberthwaite. Continue for about 1 mile to the end of the road. There is room to park to the left of the church wall. Hall Waberthwaite lies by the 'wath' or ford over the Esk. The interior of St John's Church is fascinating, retaining its early nineteenth-century box pews. Return to the main road to continue through Waberthwaite village and the ancient village of Bootle on the lower slopes of Black Combe. Follow the coast road for another 4 miles. The route now turns left **D** keeping to the A595 for Whicham.

However, there is an interesting area close by involving a detour of about 1 mile. Keep straight on along the A5093 then turn right for Silecroft. The road leads to a long sandy beach where many different types of Lake District rocks can be found.

On a clear day it is possible to see the Isle of Man.

To continue the tour follow the A595 for Broughton in Furness through Whicham. The village is the starting point for the stiff climb up Black Combe. The route now follows the Whicham valley beside the steep southern slopes of this great outcrop of Skiddaw slate which rises to a height of 1,970 feet (600 m). **Ignore all side roads and follow the A595 past Hallthwaites to turn right then left over the River Duddon at Duddon Bridge. Bear right to climb the hill to High Cross. Turn left then keep straight on for Broughton. At the market square turn left up New Street to follow the A593 for Coniston. Continue towards Lower Hawthwaite. Keep to the A593 as it bears right in the village for Torver. Follow the signs for Coniston. Drive through Torver to return to Coniston along the western side of Coniston Water.** ◼

33

WINDERMERE, THE WINSTER VALLEY AND CARTMEL

48 MILES – 3 HOURS
START AND FINISH AT WINDERMERE

From Windermere, the largest and most visited of the lakes, this tour travels to a less well known, but equally beautiful, area in the Furness fells. The route follows the Winster valley south to the coast at Grange-over-Sands. It then turns west to the historic village of Cartmel with its twelfth-century priory church known as the 'Cathedral of the Lakes'. To return to Windermere the tour follows the eastern shore of the lake for over 7 miles offering splendid opportunities for waterside picnics.

Leave Windermere along the A5074 signed for Bowness. In Bowness, pass the junction with the A592 and, shortly after, turn left for Kendal and Lancaster, still on the A5074. Continue for about 2 miles, keeping to the A5074 as it bears left at a Y-junction to run down into the Winster valley. As the road approaches Winster village look left to see its former post office, Compston House, a white-washed cottage with the date 1600 above the porch.

Continue to the crossroads in the centre of Winster and, opposite the Brown Horse Inn, turn right **A** along the minor road signposted to Bowland Bridge and Winster Church. On the left you pass the attractive village school, solidly-built of local stone and set in beautiful surroundings. It is typical of the many charming small schools scattered throughout the Lake District. The road continues down the valley to pass Winster's Holy Trinity Church, built in 1875 and half-concealed by old chestnut and beech trees.

Follow the stream through the woods to the ford beside Birks Bridge. The little River Winster widens at this point and travellers on foot can cross by the picturesque stone slab bridge. On the other side a narrow lane leads up the wooded fellside to Low Ludderburn, the house where Arthur Ransome wrote *Swallows and Amazons*. His wife, Evgenia, recalled that they were then 'in possession of the loveliest spot in the whole of the Lake District'. The house is private but walkers can follow the lane.

Continue to a T-junction. Turn left **B** for Kendal and

Bowland Bridge then, almost immediately, turn right **C** for Bowland Bridge. At the next T-junction turn right (no sign) to drive into Bowland Bridge village. Do not cross the bridge but, just past the Hare and Hounds pub, turn left for Witherslack and Grange. The road runs south down the eastern side of the Winster valley, with the river on the right.

Pass Cowmire Hall and turn right at the T-junction along the fellside road signposted to Witherslack. Shortly after passing the old houses in Pool Bank the road divides. Take the left-hand road **D** signposted to Witherslack. This climbs the fell a little and runs through beautiful oak and beech woods. After 1 mile look left for a glimpse of Witherslack Hall, now a school, but once the home of the Earl of Derby. As the road leaves the woods, you will see ahead the great limestone ramparts of Whitbarrow Scar, noted for its rare plants.

Drive past the cottages at Town End to enter

Witherslack village. Look carefully for a turning on the right signposted to Newton, Cartmel Fell and Witherslack church. **Turn right and continue for about 1 mile to see the church.** This is part of a charming group of old buildings clustered around a small green.

   Retrace the route for ¹/₄ mile, then turn right **E** for Cartmel Fell and Newton. The road runs west over the Winster valley – now widening as the river nears the sea – to a crossroads. Turn left for Lindale to follow Back o' th' Fell Road south to run under the A590. Pass the sign for Lindale village and at the junction, as you approach the village, bear right to a T-junction. Turn left for Grange and Lancaster. A few yards further on, at the crossroads in the centre of Lindale, turn right along the B5277 following the sign for Grange.

   The road runs beside woodlands to the coast of Morecambe Bay just west of Grange-over-Sands. **Keep to the main road as it bears right to**

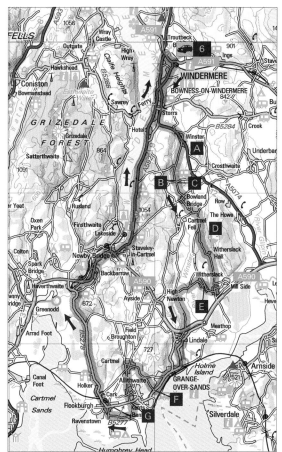

SCALE 1:250 000 OR 1 INCH TO 4 MILES *1 CM TO 2.5 KM*

follow the coast towards the town centre. Pass the junction with the B5271 and bear left to continue along the B5277 following the coast for about 1 mile. Look carefully for a turning on the right signposted to Cartmel. Turn right **F** to follow Cartmel Road for about 1½ miles to a T-junction. Following the signs for Cartmel Priory, turn right, then left to another T-junction. Turn right to drive through Cartmel village following the sign for the priory car park. Spend some time in this enchanting village if you can.

Retrace your route through the village, turning right past

Bowness-on-Windermere

the priory. Now keep straight on to the main road, cross over and head for Allithwaite. Continue for about ½ mile and, when the road bends sharply left, keep straight on down the minor road ahead

signposted to Templand. In about ½ mile, when the road bears left (to a crossroads) keep ahead down Locker Lane. Shortly after go straight over a crossroads **G** signed for Holy Well. In ¾ mile look

---

• PLACES OF INTEREST •

Windermere
The largest lake in England, Windermere runs for over 10 miles like a silver ribbon between low wooded hills, but to the north and west the lake is shadowed by the great peaks of Cumbria's highest mountains.

There are splendid views from the lakeshore but, to see the lake at its best, take the short walk which leads from the A591, opposite the information centre, to Orrest Head.

Across the lake, beyond the woods of Claife Heights, rises Coniston Old Man with the Wetherlam to the north. To the north-west Scafell rises behind Crinkle Crags followed by Bow Fell, Great Gable and the jagged outline of the Langdale Pikes. In Wordsworth's opinion, the lake could be enjoyed even more from the water.

Windermere town and its neighbour, Bowness, offer every facility for hiring boats as well as steamer tours, which ply the length of the lake from Waterhead to Lakeside.

A ferry (for foot passengers) runs across the lake from the steamer pier in Bowness and visits can be made to Belle Isle, famous for its round house.

Grange-over-Sands
Before the coming of the railway in 1857 which created the Victorian seaside resort of today, Grange, as its name suggests, was a farm for Cartmel Priory. At that time it was also a refuge for travellers as the main road from Lancaster lay across the perilous sands of Morecambe Bay. For details of walks across the sands (not to be attempted without a guide) contact the information centre in Main Street. Telephone: Grange-over-Sands (05395) 34026.

Cartmel
The Church of St Mary and St Michael was founded in 1188 and formed part of Cartmel Priory. At the Dissolution in 1537 the villagers claimed the Chapel of St Michael in the south aisle as their parish church and, although the rest of the building suffered neglect, it was restored sixty years later by George Preston of Holker Hall. He also gave the church the beautiful carved oak screen. The humour of the medieval craftsmen is revealed in some of the finely-carved misericords attached to the choir stalls. Among the oddities is a mermaid with two tails. An outstanding feature of this lovely building are two towers, one set

diagonally above the other.

The fourteenth-century priory gatehouse also survived and usually contains an exhibition of work by local artists.

Holker Hall
The superb gardens of the hall, designed by Joseph Paxton, should not be missed. They include a limestone cascade and other water features, woodland walks, rose gardens, a wildflower meadow and the world's largest sundial. The Lakeland Motor Museum is situated in the grounds. There is a cafeteria, gift shop and picnic areas. Open daily except Saturday 1 April–31 October, 10.30–6. Telephone: Newby Bridge (015395) 58328.

The Lakeside and Haverthwaite Railway
Originally, this Furness Railway branch line carried passengers and freight from Ulverston to Lakeside. Now only the 3½-mile section from Haverthwaite through Newby Bridge to Lakeside remains. Steam trains run daily along this scenic line, from 26 March– 10 April and from 30 April–30 October, and link with the lake cruisers. Telephone: Newby Bridge (015395) 31188.

left for a fine view of Wraysholme Tower, a fortified peel tower now part of a farm.

The road crosses the railway then turns right to meet the B5278. Turn right along the B5278 for Flookburgh – famous for its 'flukes', flat fish like flounders, and the quality of its Morecambe Bay shrimps.

At the crossroads in the village centre bear left, then immediately right, keeping to the B5278 signed for Holker and Ulverston. Cross the railway into Cark village. Drive through the village along the B5278 for Holker. You will see the entrance to Holker Hall and gardens on the left. This imposing mansion is the family home of Lord and Lady Cavendish and part of the building is open for visitors.

The road continues north along the foot of a steep, wooded scar with wide views over Cartmel Sands and the estuary of the River Leven to the west. **Ignore a joining road on the right and continue along the B5278**

for Haverthwaite. Cross the River Leven to a T-junction. Turn right for Newby Bridge to meet the A590. Bear right. Immediately on your left is the car park by Haverthwaite Station, the southern terminus for the Lakeside and Haverthwaite Railway. A 3-mile ride beside the River Leven takes you to Lakeside at the southern tip of Windermere.

Just after the station ignore the joining road on the left and continue along the A590 to recross the river and head north. Continue for Newby Bridge. The road runs along the east bank of the River Leven for about 2 miles to approach the village. On the left, you will see the fine sixteenth-century five-arched bridge spanning the river from which the village takes its name.

Leave the A590, to bear left along the A592. This runs along the wooded eastern shore of Windermere. You pass Fell Foot Country Park, an attractive area run by the National Trust, offering boat-launching facilities for non-

powered craft, holiday caravans and chalets, refreshments and an information centre. The road runs close to the shore and there is a lovely place for a picnic, with tables overlooking the lake, about 3 miles past Fell Foot accessed from Beech Hill car park.

There are more car parks and picnic places beside the lake as the A592 approaches Bowness-on-Windermere. **Follow the sign for the town centre past the steamer pier.**

When the A592 meets the A5074 in the centre of Bowness, bear left (signed for Ullswater and Ambleside). Turn left again still keeping to the A592 (do not follow the A5074 for Windermere) and continue along the lakeshore. The Windermere Steamboat Museum, which is well worth a visit, is on your left.

Keep on to the National Trust land at Millerground. There are car parks and splendid viewpoints. **Just beyond the last car park, Hamer Ground, turn right along the A591 to return to Windermere.** ■

A train pulls out of Haverthwaite Station on its way to Lakeside

BEATRIX POTTER COUNTRY: NEAR SAWREY, GRIZEDALE FOREST AND HAWKSHEAD

48 MILES – 3 HOURS
START AND FINISH AT WINDERMERE
ALLOW EXTRA TIME FOR A FERRY CROSSING AND VISITING HILL TOP

Between Coniston Water and Windermere lies Esthwaite Water with the small village of Near Sawrey close to its eastern shore. Here the Lake District reveals a different aspect of its character. The countryside is gentle and well wooded. Beatrix Potter described the surroundings of her home in Near Sawrey as 'very pretty hilly country, but not wild like Keswick or Ullswater'. This tour crosses Windermere by car ferry to visit Beatrix Potter's cottage, Hill Top, then runs through the Grizedale Forest to Hawkshead and Esthwaite Water before returning to Windermere via Ambleside.

From Windermere take the A591 for Ambleside. At the junction with the A592 turn left to follow this road to Bowness. The road runs close to the lakeshore with several waterside car parks, picnic places and splendid viewpoints. You pass Windermere Steamboat Museum on your right. About ¼ mile further, as you approach the junction with the A5074, you will see Rayrigg car park on the left. A signed footpath leads from the car park to the Old Laundry Visitor Centre which houses a fascinating exhibition, 'The World of Beatrix Potter'.

After the junction with the A5074 turn right to continue along the A592. Take the turning on the right, B5285, for Hawkshead via ferry. (This is a car ferry). **After ¾ mile turn right again to the ferry landing.** The ferry runs every twenty minutes throughout the year. As you cross to the beautifully wooded slopes of Claife Heights rising above the

western shore of Windermere, you pass close to Belle Isle. The circular white house on the island was built by Mr English in 1777 who sold it to the Curwen family. The island was named 'Belle Isle' after Isabella Curwen.

After landing, follow the B5285 as it curves round Ferry Nab. A car park on the right gives access to a nature trail. **Drive through Far Sawrey, keeping to the B5285, and continue to Near Sawrey.** This village was immortalised by

Beatrix Potter. Hill Top, her first home in the village, is down a short entrance on the left of the road. There is a small layby opposite, but it is better to park in the large National Trust car park 200 yards (183 m) further on. **Continue past the cottage and the Tower Bank Arms, and the turning into the car park is on the left just past a lane on the right.** (At present it is unsigned from this direction.)

To continue the tour, turn left from the car park and

Hill Top, Beatrix Potter's cottage at Near Sawrey

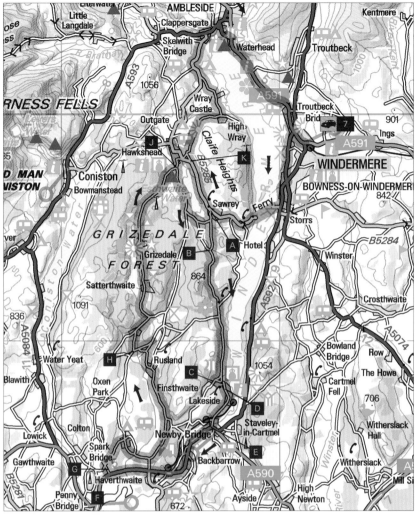

• PLACES OF INTEREST •

Windermere Steamboat Museum

This unique collection includes Beatrix Potter's rowing boat, magnificent steam launches, and an old wherry, *Ferry Boat Ann*. Trips in steam on the lake are arranged in the summer, weather permitting. Open daily Easter–October inclusive. Telephone: Windermere (015394) 45565.

Old Laundry Visitor Centre – World of Beatrix Potter

Beatrix Potter's characters come to life in three dimensions with the latest light and sound techniques.

Open daily 1 January–31 March 10–4, 1 April–30 September 10–6.30, 1 October–31 December 10–4. Telephone: Windermere (015394) 88444.

Hill Top – Near Sawrey

Born in London, a lonely child dominated by her wealthy parents, Beatrix Potter learned to love the Lake District on family holidays.

In 1896, at the age of thirty-nine, she bought Hill Top 'as an investment'. This little rough-cast farm with its animals and simple cottage garden became her retreat. Here she was

independent, and her imagination was set free to fill the house and garden with the creatures in her stories, endowing them with a life of their own.

In her will she requested that the house should not be lived in and that everything should be as she left it. So today readers of her books can recognise the details of the house she sketched so lovingly to illustrate her stories.

Hill Top is open 1 April–31 October Monday–Wednesday, Saturday and Sunday, 11–5. Telephone: Windermere (015394) 36334.

39

Grizedale Visitor Centre

The beautiful broad-leaved trees surrounding the centre were originally planted around Grizedale Hall. The hall has been pulled down. The Forestry Commission took over the 8,000-acre Grizedale Estate in 1937. The information centre contains a wildlife exhibition and a deer museum. Other facilities include an adventure playground, nine waymarked forest walks, forest sculpture, orienteering courses and four waymarked cycle routes. The centre, from which leaflets are available, is open April–October.

The centre is also the home of the Theatre-in-the-Forest which has a wide repertoire of plays, concerts (jazz and classical) and variety shows. Telephone: Satterthwaite (01229) 860291.

Hawkshead

Once a medieval wool town, Hawkshead is still charmingly seventeenth-century, with tiny squares and courts linked by narrow alley-ways. Here Wordsworth spent his happy schooldays. You can visit the old Grammar School where he carved his initials on his desk and see Ann Tyson's cottage where he lodged. North of the village is the fifteenth-century court-house, the remains of Hawkshead Manor owned by the Abbot of Furness Abbey for three hundred years. The Beatrix Potter Gallery which includes a selection of her original illustrations and a display detailing her life as an author, farmer and conservationist, is housed in the building once the office of her husband, solicitor William Heelis. The gallery is open April– October inclusive, Monday–Friday and Bank Holiday Sundays, 10.30–4.30. Telephone: Hawkshead (015394) 36355. At busy periods it is necessary to buy timed tickets.

Brockhole

The centre provides the perfect introduction to the Lake District in a glorious setting. There is something for the whole family here: lakeshore walks, formal gardens and parkland, an information centre, an adventure playground, exhibitions telling the lakeland story and a variety of special events. Open 24 March– 2 November daily 10–5.

then almost immediately turn left again down a minor road signposted to Lakeside **A**. Ignore a joining road on the right and, when the road divides, take the left-hand road **B** which runs south to cross Cunsey Beck and meet a T-junction. Turn left for Lakeside to continue south through beautiful wooded country. After about 1¹/₂ miles, as the road bears a little eastwards towards Windermere, you will see Graythwaite Hall on the right. The superb 'natural' gardens are open to the public in April, May and June when the rhododendrons and azaleas are at their best.

Ignore all joining roads and continue south in the direction of Lakeside. You pass Stott Park Bobbin Mill which is well worth a visit. Bobbin making was a flourishing local industry in the nineteenth century, and the mill has been restored to look just as it did when it was built in 1836. It is open to the public from April to October. To park, drive past the mill and take the next, rather steep, turn on the right. A sign on the left indicates the mill car park which is on your right.

Finsthwaite village is close by. Parking in the tiny village is difficult so it is better to explore on foot. Drive out of the Mill car park and turn right. At the T-junction bear left for Finsthwaite. Just past the 'Finsthwaite' sign turn right **C** up a narrow asphalted lane signposted 'Public

Footpath, High Dam'. A large National Park car park is on the right. A signed footpath leads the short distance to Finsthwaite village and St Peter's Church. In the churchyard a small stone cross marks the grave of the Finsthwaite Princess. She was Clementina Johannes Sobiesky Douglass believed to have been the illegitimate daughter of Bonny Prince Charlie. At the head of the grave an unknown hand has planted white heather!

Retrace the route past the mill car park and turn right for Lakeside **D**. From Lakeside you can take steamer trips on the lake or a return trip on the steam railway which follows the river Leven for 3¹/₂ miles to Haverthwaite. To continue the tour follow the road past the station towards Newby Bridge. Go over the railway, bear left and then, almost immediately, right to cross the bridge over the Leven.

The tour continues straight on along the A590. However, if you wish to see the little Church of St Anthony at Staveley-in-Cartmel turn immediately left along the A590 for Newby Bridge. After about ¹/₄ mile turn left on to the A592 **E** and take the first road on the right signed for Staveley church. At the T-junction turn right into Chapel House Wood. This church stands alone on the right of the road. It was built by local farmers in 1504 and has fine carved box pews, a three-decker pulpit and some fifteenth-century stained glass including a picture of St Anthony and his pig. Retrace your route towards Newby Bridge, turning left along the A592 and right when this road meets the A590 in the village. The tour continues on the A590 which, at first, follows the east bank of the Leven.

Ignore the first bridge over the river and continue along the A590 to cross the Leven to Haverthwaite Station. Keep straight on in the direction of Greenodd. Go straight over the first crossroads and continue to go across the bridge over Rusland Pool.

After about ¹/₂ mile turn right **F** for Bouth. In ¹/₄ mile turn right **G** and keep on for almost 1 mile to Bouth. The road turns right, signposted to Finsthwaite and Rusland, and heads south over Rusland Pool. Over the causeway bear left for Rusland driving north along the Rusland valley.

When the road divides continue for Rusland along the left-hand road signposted to Satterthwaite and Grange. On either side are the beautiful Rusland Woods. **The road turns left signposted to Oxen Park, then right past Rusland Hall gatehouse.** Rusland church stands high on the fellside ahead. **Turn right following the sign for the church, then left at the T-junction to the church itself where there is roadside parking. The road bears left in front of Rusland church.** Arthur Ransome and his wife Evgenia are buried, as he requested, in the churchyard.

With the church on your left, continue down the lane to rejoin the road. Bear right, cross Force Beck and, a little further on, turn right for Satterthwaite **H. After ¹/₂ mile bear right again and in Force Mills turn left for Satterthwaite.** The road runs through Grizedale Forest with glorious places to picnic and

Evening sunlight on the grave of Arthur Ransome and his wife Evgenia in the churchyard which overlooks the Rusland valley

forest trails to follow. **Continue through Satterthwaite village to one of the most delightful at Bogle Crag.**

Follow the road as it heads north to Grizedale village. Here the Forestry Commission have established a visitor centre which gives a splendid introduction to the wildlife of the area. **Continue following the signs for Hawkshead. Turn left at the T-junction **J**, follow the road as it turns right, then turn left following the signs to Hawkshead car park.** This picturesque village must be explored on foot.

Retrace the route to **J and keep straight on to drive down the western shore of Esthwaite Water in the direction of Lakeside. At the Y-junction take the left-hand road for Near Sawrey.** A car park near the lake's southern tip gives access to the waterside. **At the next Y-junction turn left to meet the B5285 in Near Sawrey. Turn left in the**

direction of Hawkshead to drive north along the eastern shore of Esthwaite Water. **When the road turns left for Hawkshead, turn right along a minor road signposted to Wray **K**. Ignore the first road on the left. The road bends right for a few yards then left to run north past the Latterbarrow.** The road runs high along the fellside giving a fine view of lonely Blelham Tarn cradled in the valley below. Continue through High Wray past the vicarage, once the home of Canon Rawnsley, one of the founders of the National Trust. He became a great friend of Beatrix Potter, whom he met while she was on holiday at nearby Wray Castle. He suggested that she should submit the manuscript of *The Tale of Peter Rabbit* to Frederick Warne and Company who became her publisher.

When the road meets the B5286 turn right for Ambleside. When this road meets the A593 turn right again for Ambleside. Cross the bridge, turn left then right for Windermere and follow the road past Waterhead to meet the A591. Turn right to follow this road down the eastern shore of Windermere. After about 2 miles you pass Brockhole, the Lake District National Park Visitor Centre.

Keep to the A591 as it crosses the A592 to return to Windermere. ■

The fisherman's lake – Esthwaite Water

SIX LAKES AND 'BACK O' SKIDDAW'

75 MILES – 4 HOURS
START AND FINISH AT WINDERMERE

This tour is ideal if your time in the Lake District is limited. It offers splendid views of six lakes and there is an opportunity to explore the most remote part of the Lake District National Park, a quiet area of undulating moorland to the north known as 'Back o' Skiddaw'. Although the route crosses the highest pass in the Lake District, Kirkstone, this normally presents few difficulties, but beware early snowfalls.

Leave Windermere along the A591 in the direction of Ambleside. Cross the A592 and continue along the A591 beside the lake. After crossing Troutbeck Bridge, turn right to follow Bridge Lane. This winds up the valley with the stream on the right.

Troutbeck village is composed of scattered groups of houses built around the wells which, until recently, served as their water supply.

After about 1 mile a minor road joins on the left. Overlooking the junction is one of Lakeland's treasures, Town

End. **To find the car park, turn left up the minor road and, after a few yards, turn right into an entry leading past a gate (unsigned at present).** Town End was the home of the Browne family, well-to-do yeomen or 'statesmen (originally estatesmen) from about 1626 to 1943. It has remained unaltered for three hundred years. Now owned by the National Trust it is open to the public.

Continue along the valley through the village to meet the A592. Turn left to ascend Kirkstone Pass surrounded by thrilling mountain views. Continue along the A592 as it runs over the summit of the pass. A panoramic view of Patterdale and the Ullswater fells is revealed. There is a car park on the left. The road descends to the eastern shore of Brothers Water. A footpath leads from the car park north of this peaceful lake to the waterside.

Continue along the A592 through Patterdale. This was originally St Patrick's Dale, named after the saint who, according to tradition, was shipwrecked on Duddon Sands and made his way to this valley.

A steamer leaves Glenridding pier on Ullswater

Carry on along the western shore of Ullswater towards Glenridding. After about ¼ mile look for St Patrick's Well on the left, which is said to have healing powers. The former lead mining village of Glenridding is now a tourist centre and the Ullswater Steamers *Raven* and *Lady of the Lake* operate from the pier. There is a National Park Information Centre in the car park where you can see a reconstruction of a mine shaft.

Keep to the A592 as it hugs the western shore of Ullswater. Just past the junction with the A5091 A, you will see the car park for one of Cumbria's most spectacular waterfalls, Aira Force, on your left.

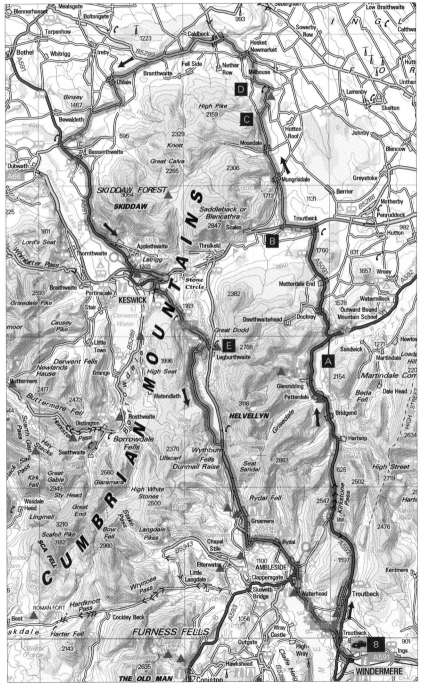

SCALE 1:250 000 OR 1 INCH TO 4 MILES 1 CM TO 2.5 KM

The tour follows the A5091 after a visit to the falls.
A footpath from the falls leads to Gowbarrow Park where there is a memorial seat on the top of Yew Crag giving wonderful lake views.

Return to the junction with the A5091 and turn right to climb Park Brow and drive through Matterdale. In just over 1 1/2 miles look for a minor road signposted to Penruddock on the right, beside which there is room to park. The entrance to Matterdale church is close by. This was built by local craftsmen in 1685. It is a typical lakeland church with a low-pitched slate roof and ancient beams. From the seat outside there is a view over Place Fell to the High Street mountain range.

Continue to the junction with the A66 and turn left in the direction of Keswick. Ignore the first unsignposted right turn and continue for about 1 1/4 miles to take the second minor road on the right signposted to Mungrisdale village and Caldbeck  B. This leads north beside the River Glenderamackin with the steep slopes of Souther Fell beneath the saddle-shaped summit of Blencathra rising to the west.

A 'statesman's house, Town End, in Troubeck

When the river bears left the road continues into the small village of Mungrisdale. The Church of St Kentigern (also called St Mungo) contains a seventeenth-century, three-decker pulpit. There is also a memorial to Raisley Calvert whose bequest to Wordsworth, who had nursed him during his last illness, made it possible for the poet to retire and devote his time to writing.

Drive along the foot of the steep fellside to Bowscale. As you approach the village you will see a parking area beside the road. From here you can follow the bridleway sign just before the first house in the village to Bowscale Tarn, hidden away below the 500-foot- (152 m) high wall of Bowscale Fell. It is an easy walk, about 2 miles round.

Cross the River Caldew, and continue through Mosedale along the foot of Carrock Fell. The unfenced road winds over open moors with long restful views. **After about 1 1/4 miles the road divides. Bear right C and continue to a T-junction. Turn left to cross a bridge following the sign for Hesket Newmarket and Caldbeck. The road now becomes fenced and turns west to run to a T-junction with Pasture Lane. Turn right D following the Hesket Newmarket sign to meet the main road. Bear left to drive into Hesket Newmarket.**

• PLACES OF INTEREST •

Troutbeck
Nearly all of the cottages and barns date from the seventeenth and early eighteenth century and the whole village is a conservation area.

Town End is built on the traditional 'statesman's plan', divided into two basic units, the main living room, or 'firehouse' where the cooking would be done over an open hearth in an inglenook, and the 'downhouse' which would act as a scullery, a fuel store and brewhouse. The house is a fascinating reminder of times past, but what makes the house unique is its contents. The Brownes were not only good

farmers, they were excellent craftsmen and threw nothing away. Town End is furnished with their beautiful carved woodwork and contains a marvellous collection of books, papers and domestic implements. Outside is a typical lakeland bank barn, set into the hillside. The upper floor, generally used for threshing, was entered from the fields and the lower floor gave onto the farm yard. The open-fronted spinning-gallery is also typical of old lakeland farms.

Open 1 April–30 October Tuesday– Friday, Sundays and Bank Holiday Mondays 1–5. Telephone: Ambleside (015394) 32628.

Bowscale Tarn
The tarn's dramatic setting has inspired a local saying that the water is so deep and dark it reflects the stars even on sunny days. There is also a legend that in its depths live two giant trout that will never die.

Carrock Fell
The Lake District is well-known as a rich source of minerals and this fell is a mecca for geologists. Composed of volcanic rock, it contains more that twenty types of minerals including tungsten ores which were mined for use in specialised steels.

At the top of the village street keep to the main road as it turns right for Caldbeck. In a little over 1¹/₂ miles you reach this attractive village whose most famous resident was the huntsman, John Peel.

Drive through Caldbeck to meet the B5299. Continue along this road as it runs over the rolling moorland of Back o' Skiddaw through Parkend. From Parkend continue for about 1 mile, ignore a turning on the right for Carlisle and, shortly after when the B5299 bears right for Aspatria, keep straight on for Uldale. On the left waves of moorland ripple south to the rounded slopes of Skiddaw. The road climbs a little and, at the highest point, look west for a magnificent view over the Cumbrian coastal plain and the Solway Firth to the Scottish Southern Uplands.

A pleasant diversion can be made after descending into Uldale. This village is the setting of David's house in Hugh Walpole's novel *Rogue Herries*. At the crossroads in Uldale turn left along a minor road signposted to Over Water and Orthwaite to meet a T-junction. Bear right, following the sign for Bassenthwaite and Keswick. Continue along the north bank of a very pretty tarn, Over Water, to meet the road south of Uldale. Turn left for Keswick and continue to meet the A591. Turn left for Bassenthwaite to take the A591 which runs along the eastern side of Bassenthwaite Lake.

The road runs between the lake and woodlands and after about 3 miles you will see Dodd car park and picnic place on the left. Forest trails lead from the car park, and a short but stiff climb brings you to Dodd summit, a magnificent viewpoint. Opposite is the entrance to Mirehouse, an attractive eighteenth-century

• PLACES OF INTEREST •

Hesket Newmarket
A most attractive village of colour-washed cottages facing a sloping green. From 1747 to 1900 the village was important for its market, and on the green is a roofed remnant of its old market cross. In the road close by is an iron bull-ring. At the top of the street stands Hesket Hall, a gable-winged seventeenth-century farm house, cruciform in shape and said to have been designed as a giant sundial.

Caldbeck
John Peel was born at Park End, Caldbeck in 1776 and his grave, appropriately decorated with hunting horns, is in the churchyard. The village was formerly a busy place, involved in bobbin, cloth and clog-making, brewing, farming and mining. Today clogs are still made in the village. Close to the church is Priests Mill, a restored water-mill housing an interesting mining museum.

Bassenthwaite Lake
This lake is protected by the Lake District Special Planning Board in order to conserve wildlife. Over seventy bird species breed along the lake's shores. However, a pleasant walk known as the Allerdale Ramble traces the eastern shore. The best place to start is Dodd car park.

Mirehouse
The earliest part of this manor house, beautifully sited beside Bassenthwaite Lake, dates from

the seventeenth century. The Spedding family, who still own the house, were noted for their hospitality. Among their many literary guests was Alfred, Lord Tennyson, who composed part of *Morte D'Arthur* in the grounds. Open 30 March–30 October. House: Sundays, Wednesdays and Bank Holiday Mondays (also Fridays in August) 2–4.30. Grounds, tearoom and playgrounds: daily 10.30–5.30. Telephone: Keswick (017687) 72287.

house with literary connections. It is open to the public.

Bear left at the A66 roundabout north of Keswick for Penrith and Windermere. Continue for about 1 mile to cross the River Greta. Now rejoin the A591 as it turns left to loop round the A66 for Windermere. In ¹/₄ mile turn left, still following the A591, for Windermere. Keep on for about 4 miles, then turn right **E** down a minor road signposted to Thirlmere. Cross the dam and bear left along the scenic road which hugs the western shore of Thirlmere. The road meets the A591 at the southern end of the lake. Turn right to climb Dunmail Raise. As the road descends on the other side

there are glorious views over Grasmere vale.

To visit Grasmere village turn right down the B5287. Dove Cottage, where Wordsworth composed some of his greatest poems, is beside the A591 on your left.

Keep to the A591 as it skirts the northern shore of Rydal Water. Continue to drive through Ambleside to reach the shore of Windermere at Waterhead. Now the A591 continues south along Windermere's eastern shore. You pass the entrance to the Lake District National Park Visitor Centre at Brockhole on the right. Keep to the A591 as it crosses Troutbeck Bridge and returns to Windermere. ■

SCOUT SCAR AND KENTMERE

45 MILES – 2½ HOURS
START AND FINISH AT KENDAL

The limestone fells around Kendal and the Lyth valley may lack some of the drama of the mountain peaks to the west and north, but this attractive landscape of winding lanes, low hills and scattered woodlands interrupted by sheer-sided ridges or scars richly repays exploration. This tour climbs to the top of Scout Scar, a magnificent viewpoint, before following the Kentmere valley into the heart of the mountains of the High Street range. The return route crosses the Skelsmergh fells to run beside the River Mint back to Kendal. Allow plenty of time for the Kentmere valley – a round trip of about 7 miles – as the road is narrow with passing places.

The magnificent east window in Staveley church

The tour starts from the top of Highgate, halfway down the main street in Kendal. Following the one-way system north, turn left **A** down Allhallows Lane (unsigned). The turning is directly opposite the town hall. This building houses the clearly signed information centre. **The road** runs west to a junction. Bear left along Beast Banks. Castle Howe is on your left. Keep ahead up Greenside following the sign for Underbarrow. The town is soon left behind as the road crosses the eastern boundary of the Lake District National Park and bridges the A591. After ¾ mile the road climbs to the dip between the wooded slopes of Scout Scar to the south and Cunswick Scar to the north.

Just after the crest look carefully for a car park signed on the right. This is the park for Scout Scar, and a few minutes' walk is rewarded by a magnificent view. Cross the road and follow the footpath sign on the left to the top of the Scar. Looking east, Kendal lies cradled in the Kent

· *PLACES OF INTEREST* ·

Kendal
Kendal is a fascinating town, steeped in history. It lies either side of the river in the shallow valley of the River Kent with a backcloth of limestone fells. Most of the buildings are grey limestone which have led to Kendal being called 'The Auld Grey Town'. Castle Howe, to the west of the town, is the site of an eleventh-century Norman castle. The ruins of a thirteenth-century castle, the birthplace of Henry VIII's last wife, Katherine Parr, can be seen on the other side of the river on Castle Hill. The woollen industry was established here by Flemish weavers and flourished for six hundred years. So important was this industry that it gave Kendal its town motto 'Wool is my bread'. It was noted for the production of 'Kendal Green', a woollen cloth worn by archers. Workers were housed in the many courts reached by narrow alleyways which are an intriguing feature of the town.

Today, Kendal is an important communications centre and a busy market town. Modern activities include engineering and insurance, but the traditional industries still thrive: carpets, shoes, hornware, brush and rope making, the manufacture of snuff and, of course, the production of the famous mint cake.

Kendal Museum features wildlife dioramas and a collection of Alfred Wainwright memorabilia. Opening times vary. Telephone: Kendal (01539) 721374. Old ways are captured in eighteenth-century Abbot Hall which houses the Museum of Lakeland Life and Industry and an Art Gallery. Telephone: (01539) 722464. Markets are held on Wednesdays and Saturdays.

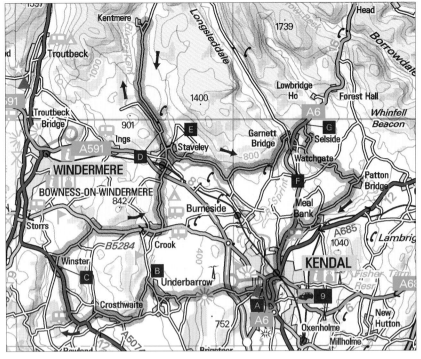

valley with the rolling outline of
the Pennines beyond; to the west
is a panorama of the Lakeland
fells and to the south Morecambe
Bay. The little shelter on the
ridge was erected in 1912 to
commemorate the coronation
of George V.

The road descends to the
foot of Scout Scar and continues
across the northern end of the

Lyth valley which is threaded by
the River Gilpin and many smaller
streams. (There is no River Lyth).
**Pass a turning on the left and,
when the road bears left to
a T-junction, turn right
following the sign for
Crosthwaite and Bowland
Bridge. The road kinks left
again just after you pass the
'Underbarrow' village sign.**

**Turn right opposite the
Punch Bowl Inn** (a sixteenth-
century coaching Inn) **following
the sign for Crook. The
road bears right to enter
Underbarrow village. Leave
the road to drive straight
ahead and park by the
church.** Several delightful
footpaths lead from the village,
crossing tiny bridges over the

Kendal's elegant eighteenth-century Abbot Hall

47

Underbarrow

The old houses of this village are widely spread in lovely countryside at the head of the Lyth valley. The area is noted for its wild flowers which include fields full of daffodils and lilies of the valley. In a charming setting beside Chapel Beck is the Church of All Saints which retains its old oil lamps. The Lyth valley to the south is flat and fen-like but should be visited in the spring when the fruit trees are in blossom. Lyth valley damsons have a different 'nutty' flavour.

Staveley

Industry has left its mark on the architecture of Staveley. Situated beside the River Kent, the presence of a good water supply led to the development of cotton as well as woollen mills. There was always a great demand for bobbins and Staveley was once the centre of the bobbin-turning industry. Today, the Staveley Woodturning Company still produces turned tool handles, and local craftsmen make traditional furniture in solid oak and ash.

If possible visit the church. The magnificent east window was designed by Burne-Jones and depicts angels against a vibrant deep blue background.

Kentmere

Kentmere Hall dates from the fourteenth century and for twelve generations was the home of the Gilpin family, one of whose members is remembered as the killer of the last wild boar in England in 1325.

Dyer's yellow broom which was added to the blue from woad to produce the famous 'Kendal Green' still grows in the valley. When the lake was drained a Viking spearhead and a medieval canoe were found. Deposits of clay in the lakebed are now quarried for use in industry.

marked only with a preaching cross from which the village takes its name. **Follow the road through the village past the post office and bear left to the junction with the A5074. Keep straight ahead along the A5074 signed for Winster and Windermere. Keep to the main road as it turns right signed for Bowness.** The road runs north to Winster through a tumbled countryside of low crags and gorse-covered slopes. **At the crossroads in Winster, turn right just before the Brown Horse pub on your left. The lane runs uphill. Bear right at the top, keeping to the lane as it dips past attractive Knipe Tarn.** The tarn is particularly lovely in summer with its tiny island ringed with white water-lilies. **Ignore a joining road on the right and continue to meet the B5284. Turn right for Crook.**

After 1$\frac{1}{2}$ miles you pass the pub and post office in Crook. **Take the next road on the left for Staveley.** The road heads north to this large village, once a busy industrial centre. It lies at the foot of high fells where the River Gowan meets the River Kent. **Cross the A591 and continue through Staveley following the signs for**

streams arising from springs at the head of the valley. Pamphlets with details of these are available in the church.

Return to the road and continue for Crook past the old school. Take the first turning on the left, Broom Lane . The lane heads south through rocky outcrops to a T-junction. Turn right in the direction of Crosthwaite. Before the village you pass the Church of St Mary on the left. Many churches have been built on this site which was originally

Garnett Bridge over the River Sprint at the foot of Longsleddale

48

Looking down on the River Kent from Barley Bridge

Kentmere. The road runs past the church to the west bank of the River Kent. Barley Bridge is on your right. You pass a late-eighteenth-century stone-built cotton mill, complete with clock and bell tower. This is now a paper-packaging factory.

High crags rise on either side as the road follows the west bank of the river, north. In just under ½ mile turn right to cross the river following the sign for Kentmere **D**. Continue along the east bank of the river as the valley cuts deeper into the High Street mountain range. You pass Millriggs at the foot of Kentmere Tarn. This narrow strip of water is the remains of a lake which, before it was drained, filled the valley south of Kentmere. Sheep-dog trials are held at Millriggs on the last Thursday in September. **Follow the road as it bears left to cross the River Kent to Kentmere village.** There is a small car park here. Surrounded by some of the finest fells in the Lake District, this lovely spot is an ideal place for a short walk and a picnic.

Retrace the route down the valley turning right over the bridge to continue down the western bank of the river. This time do not continue into Staveley but instead, by the mill, turn left over Barley Bridge **E**. Turn right for Burneside. Follow the road along the east bank of the river to a Y-junction. Take the right-hand road which at first runs through woods beside the Kent, and then runs south to a T-junction. Turn left and follow the road as it winds along the fellside in the direction of Garnett Bridge. When the road meets the next T-junction turn left to trace the west bank of the River Sprint to the attractive little village of Garnett Bridge at the foot of Longsleddale. This is where John Cunliffe's Postman Pat delivers the mail. Today it is difficult to imagine a quieter valley, but in the eighteenth century Longsleddale was threaded by a busy pack-horse trail from Kendal. The route continued over the Gatesgarth Pass and down into the Haweswater valley.

Cross the bridge and turn right **F** for Shap and Penrith. Follow the road along the east bank of the River Sprint and meet the main road (A6). Turn left for Penrith. After about ¾ mile turn right **G** for Selside, church and school. Drive down to the church where there is roadside parking. Pictures inside trace the development of this typical small lakeland church through the ages. The Elizabethan farmhouse in the valley on the right was originally Selside Hall and is built around a fourteenth-century peel tower.

From the church continue down the lane. Bear right past Selside Farm and keep on to a T-junction. Turn left and continue past Poppy Farm. Drive straight over the crossroads and follow the lane to the T-junction at Patton Bridge. The bridge crosses the River Mint on the left. Do not cross the bridge but turn right to drive through lovely countryside. The fells roll gently down to the wooded banks of the river on your left and ahead Kendal lies half-concealed beside the Kent. The road descends the fellside to run closer to the river and curves round the mill at Meal Bank. **Ignore a turning on the left to a bridge and keep straight on along Helme Lane with the river on your left. At the junction with the A6 turn left for Kendal. Follow the A6 over Mint Bridge and under the railway to return to the town centre.** ■

KIRKBY LONSDALE, SILVERDALE AND ARNSIDE

50 MILES – 2¹/₂ HOURS
START AND FINISH AT KENDAL

This tour runs south to the Lune valley to visit the charming small market town of Kirkby Lonsdale. It then heads west towards Morecambe Bay and the Silverdale peninsula south of the Kent estuary. This lovely countryside, characterised by wooded hills sheltering stone-built villages, is famous for its nature reserves and has been designated an Area of Outstanding Natural Beauty.

Leave Kendal town centre heading south along the A65 signed at first for Skipton. About ³/₄ mile after crossing the river take the road on the left signed for Oxenholme, the B6254 **A**. The road bends to cross the railway. Keep to the B6254 (ignore sign for Oxenholme village). This is limestone country and the road winds around small steep-sided fells threaded by many tiny streams. After running through Old Hutton the B6254 goes under the motorway to continue south through gentler countryside. **Drive through Old Town keeping to the B6254 following the sign for Kirkby Lonsdale.** Ahead there are beautiful views over the Lune valley to the hills of the Yorkshire Dales.

The road descends into the Lune valley to enter Kirkby Lonsdale. Keep to the B6254 as it bends right then left round the church. Another right turn allows the road to resume its southerly heading to the market place. This is a good place to park (on Thursday, market day, use one of the other car parks) as Kirkby Lonsdale is best explored on foot. It is a delightful little town with a jumble of narrow cobbled streets lined with old houses, many dating from the sixteenth century. **Past the market place the road continues to a junction with the A65. Turn left for a few yards, then right B heading south, still following the B6254 for Whittington and Carnforth.** This takes you along the west side of the Lune valley

After passing the first houses in Whittington the B6254 turns left . Leave the B6254 here and bear right following the sign for Hutton Roof C. Pass the church and keep ahead to follow the road as it bears right at a fork and heads west to a Y-junction. Continue along the left-hand road past Hutton Roof quarries in the direction of Burton-in-Kendal. Ignore the turning for Hutton Roof village. The road runs just south of the steep, wooded slopes of Dalton Crags and past Dalton Park. **At a T-junction turn left,**

• PLACES OF INTEREST •

Kirkby Lonsdale
Standing high on a bank overlooking the River Lune, this fascinating town built of pale gold limestone has been the market and social centre for the Lune valley since the thirteenth century. It contains the finest Norman church in Cumbria. St Mary's, built on an Anglo-Saxon site, was restored in 1866 but retains many original features, including the three westernmost arches and piers of the nave's north arcade and the south and west doorways. A stone plaque beside the west porch indicates the path to 'Ruskin's View' across the island in the Lune to the hills beyond. Tempted by Turner's painting, John Ruskin visited the town in 1857. Enchanted by this view John Ruskin wrote ' The valley of the Lune at Kirkby Lonsdale is one of the loveliest scenes in England... whatever moorland hill, and sweet river, and English forest foliage can be at their best is gathered here'. Close by, the Radical Steps lead down to the riverside where a footpath follows the riverbank south to the Devil's Bridge. The three graceful arches spanning the river are probably thirteenth-century. Its origin is obscure but according to legend this magnificent bridge was one night's work for the devil!

Two miles south-east of the town is Cowan Bridge on the River Leck, formerly the site of the clergy daughters' school featured in Charlotte Bronte's *Jane Eyre*. Kirkby Lonsdale is the 'Lowood' of the novel.

then, after a few yards, turn right following the sign for Yealand. The road crosses the M6, the Lancaster Canal and the railway. **Continue straight over the next crossroads following the sign for Yealand to a T-junction in Yealand**

Redmayne. Turn left to follow the road running along the foot of a high, wooded ridge to Yealand Conyers. In about 1½ miles, as you enter the village, take the turning to Leighton Hall on the right. The road climbs the ridge to

descend to the lodge at the entrance of the drive leading to Leighton Hall, beautifully sited in a natural amphitheatre among the fells. Here there is a superb view over the sands of Morecambe Bay to the Furness hills. The hall is open to the public.

The Lancaster canal near Yealand Redmayne

The road turns south beside Warton Crag to a T-junction. **Turn right**  **signposted to Carnforth along the road through Warton village past the church.** The mainly fifteenth-century church has connections with the Washington family (ancestors of George Washington) who lived in the area. The last of the family was vicar here from 1799 to 1823. **Continue in the direction of Carnforth, but at the junction take the right-hand road**  **that runs down to the coast of Morecambe Bay.**

Steam railway enthusiasts should make a short detour at the this junction. **Take the left-hand road and in ³/₄ mile Carnforth Steamtown Railway Museum is on the right.**

At the coast **the road turns right to run north close to the** shore with Warton Crag rising steeply on the right. The views are magnificent as you approach the inlet of Leighton Moss. This is a wilderness of reed-beds and waterways dividing the fells of Yealand Redmayne from Silverdale, the small wooded peninsula you will see ahead. **The road bends left to cross the mouth of the reserve and goes over a railway to a T-junction. Turn right past a joining road on the left. Keep ahead for a few yards to a junction just before the railway. Turn right**  **over the railway bridge following the sign for Leighton Moss Nature Reserve.** The Reserve Visitor Centre is immediately on your right. The reserve is open throughout the year and information and permits can be obtained from the centre.

Continue beside the reserve to a T-junction at Yealand Storrs. Turn left following the sign for Beetham and Arnside. Keep ahead, following the signs for Silverdale, along the main road as it bears south towards Silverdale village. Cross the railway to a T-junction and turn right. There is a car park on the right which gives access to Eaves Wood Nature Reserve.

Leave the main road as it turns left for Silverdale village and bear right  **following the sign for Arnside. The road runs to the coast beside the sands of Morecambe Bay and then turns right.** In ³/₄ mile you pass to the left of Arnside Tower, a five-storey peel tower dating from the fifteenth century.

Ruskin's view over the River Lune from Kirkby Lonsdale

The road runs round Arnside Knott and down the steep street in Arnside village. Bear left, following the sign to the promenade to reach the seafront. There is parking near the pier. There are many delightful coastal and woodland walks from the village. The short walk up Arnside Knott is rewarded by a magnificent view of the Lakeland hills and the northern Pennines. The beehive-shaped building is a monument to Queen Victoria.

Turn right  along the coastal road, B5282, to follow the seafront. Bear left, for Milnthorpe, under the railway. Continue along the B5282 to cross the small stone bridge over the River Bela and head east to the crossroads in Milnthorpe. You may like to make a short detour here to visit the historic village of Beetham and its restored eighteenth-century Heron Corn Mill.

Turn right at the crossroads to follow the A6 along the east bank of the Bela and cross the bridge into the village. Just over the bridge there is a car park on the right and a footpath to the mill.

Retrace the route to the crossroads in Milnthorpe. Turn right along the B6385 for Crooklands and keep ahead, ignoring all side roads. Continue over the railway and cross a tributary of the River Bela at Rowell Bridge. Follow the road over the A590 heading for Crooklands. The road turns right beside the Lancaster canal. Bear left over Crooklands Bridge to the A65 and turn left along the A65 through Crooklands village.

Follow the A65 through Endmoor, keeping to the main road (left-hand road) at the fork in the village. The road runs north towards Oxenholme past the southern tip of The Helm, a prominent ridge of Silurian rock, 605 feet (184 m) above sea level, crowned with the remains of a Roman fort.

About 3 miles after leaving Endmoor, make a short detour to see Natland. The turning to this attractive village is on the left. Natland green has welcoming seats and is ringed by old houses.

Opposite the green turn right past the church then right again to return to the A65. Turn left along the A65 to return to the centre of Kendal. ■

SIZERGH CASTLE, LEVENS HALL AND THE SOUTHERN LAKES

50 MILES – 4 HOURS
START AND FINISH AT KENDAL

There is a great deal to enjoy on this interesting tour. After visits to two splendid stately homes with beautiful gardens set among the limestone scars of Cumbria, the route crosses into the Lake District National Park to follow the shores of Coniston Water and Esthwaite Water. Windermere is crossed by car ferry, and a quiet road over the fells leads back to Kendal.

Leave Kendal on the A6 signed for Lancaster, heading south down the valley of the River Kent. When the A6 meets the A591 keep ahead along the A591 for Lancaster. At the next roundabout leave the A591 and turn left along the A590 signed for Barrow, Sizergh Castle and Levens Hall. The A590 loops under the A591 and you will see the sign for Sizergh Castle almost immediately on your right. Turn right **A** to visit this splendid, predominantly Elizabethan, house.

To continue the tour return to the A590 and head west for about ¼ mile. Turn left along the A6 following the sign for Levens Hall. Keep ahead for about 1 mile to a junction. Bear a little left here to cross Levens Bridge and immediately on your right you will see the entry to Levens Hall. This beautiful Elizabethan house is famous for its topiary gardens and is also

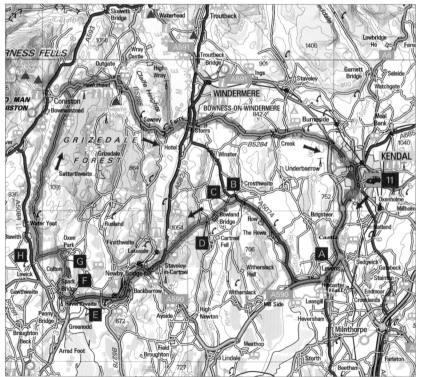

SCALE 1:250 000 OR 1 INCH TO 4 MILES *1 CM TO 2.5 KM*

open to the public.

Return to the A6, turning left to recross Levens Bridge, then immediately left again to rejoin the A590 and ontinue following the signs for Barrow. The road runs along a causeway over the flat Lyth valley – a rich fruit-growing area, brilliant with blossom in the spring – towards the River Gilpin and the eastern boundary of the National Park. **In just over 1 mile, after passing the Gilpin Bridge Inn, turn right along the A5074 following the sign for Bowness and Windermere.** The great limestone escarpment of Whitbarrow Scar rises steeply on the left, and across the valley are the less formidable ridges of Burnbarrow Scar and Scout Scar.

Keep to the main A5074 as it winds north past farms and hamlets before bearing left to leave the Lyth valley. After about 5 miles turn left

Looking across Windermere to Lakeside from Fell Foot

B following the minor road that runs through Tarnside to High Birks. Turn left C following the sign for Bowland Bridge. The road descends into the Winster valley to cross the river at Bowland Bridge. Lovely views of this pleasantly undulating valley dotted with small woods unfold. **The road continues past a turning on the left and then turns right to a fork by the Mason's Arms pub. Keep along the main road – left at the fork D. The road climbs Strawberry Bank and turns left round Cawker How. Ignore the joining road on the right at Lightwood and keep on as the road descends the fells and bears left past Gummers How.** Close to the highest point of the fell the gleam of Windermere appears ahead. Stop in Gummers How car park on the left to enjoy the magnificent view. It is an ideal spot for a picnic.

Continue to the junction with the A592, near the southern tip of the lake at Fell Foot, where the route turns left for Newby Bridge. If you would like to picnic, hire a rowing boat or just stroll by the water's edge, Fell Foot Country Park close by is the perfect place. The park also has a café.

To continue the tour follow the A592 to its junction with

• *PLACES OF INTEREST* •

Sizergh Castle
The oldest part of this grey, winged house is the massive peel tower, nearly 60 feet (18 m) high with walls 9-foot- (2.7 m) thick at the base. In 1450 a Great Hall was added, and a century later two wings containing workshops and kitchens were built on at right angles. The Great Hall was enlarged at the same time and decorated with fine panelling and superbly carved overmantels. Alterations to the exterior of the house were made in the eighteenth century, but the interior has remained little changed. Although the castle now belongs to the National Trust it has been the home of the Strickland family for more than 750 years and the family still live in the north wing. The Stricklands were staunch supporters of the Stuart cause and the house contains a large collection of Stuart portraits and relics, including a two-handed sword dating from 1340.

The house is surrounded by terraces and gardens, especially beautiful in autumn. They include the Trust's largest limestone rock garden. Open 3 April–31 October Sunday–Thursday 1.30–5.30. Closed Good Friday. Telephone: Sedgwick (015395) 60070.

Levens Hall
Beautifully situated on the banks of the River Kent, Levens Hall is one of the finest Elizabethan mansions in Cumbria. The peel tower and hall were acquired by the Bellingham family in the sixteenth century. They transformed the building, decorating the interior with magnificent oak panelling and plastered ceilings. The topiary garden dates from the seventeenth century and was designed by Beaumont, a pupil of Le Notre. Open 3 April–30 September Sunday–Thursday 11–5. Telephone: Sedgwick (015395) 60321.

Levens Hall seen from its famous topiary gardens

the A590 in Newby Bridge. **Turn right along the A590 as it traces the southern bank of the River Leven.** After leaving the village you will see the sixteenth-century five-arched bridge over the river from which the village takes its name.

Keep to the A590 past the turning for Backbarrow to cross the River Leven in the direction of Haverthwaite. Just past a joining road on the right you will see the sign for Haverthwaite Station. This is the southern terminus for the Lakeside and Haverthwaite steam railway offering an opportunity for a 4-mile steam train ride.

From the station continue along the A590 over the B5278 heading west over the Rusland valley. Ignore the first road signed for Bouth on the right and continue over the river, Rusland Pool. After ½ mile leave the A590 and turn right following the second sign for Bouth **E**. **Shortly the road meets a T-junction. Turn left in the direction of Spark Bridge F. After ½ mile, at the crossroads, turn right for Oxen Park.** The road runs through glorious countryside past Colton. **Continue north following the sign for Satterthwaite. In Oxen Park village take the first left turn G signposted to Bandrake Head, Lowick and Nibthwaite. Follow the minor road as it turns left over Colton Beck for Bandrake Head. In Bandrake Head ignore a turning on the left and keep on following the sign for Lowick and Coniston along Bessy Bank Lane.** This lane runs through woods to descend steeply to the eastern bank of the River Crake. **Turn right H to follow the road which winds along the eastern bank of the river towards the foot of Coniston Water.**

The road runs through High Nibthwaite where Arthur Ransome

Colton, set in splendid walking country

Colton

This small village is set in lovely countryside between the Rusland valley and the River Crake and is a good centre for walks. Follow the track above the village to visit Holy Trinity Church which dates from the fifteenth century. The hillside above is a fine viewpoint.

Belle Isle

The Romans were the first to settle on this romantic island covering thirty-eight acres. In the early eighteenth century the Philipson family had a home there. During the 1745 rebellion the royalist

Major Robert Philipson was beseiged on the island for eight days by Colonel Briggs and his Roundheads. When rescued, the Major rode into Kendal church, where the Colonel was at prayer, seeking revenge. The congregation chased the Major out with so much vigour that he was forced to leave his helmet and sword behind. These can be seen today in the church.

The round house which stands on this prominent site today, invited a great deal of criticism at the time it was built. Wordsworth disliked it intensely, but had to

admit that it was the first house to be built in the Lake District for the sake of the scenery. Thomas English, for whom the house was erected, left it disheartened, and ultimately it was bought by Isabella Curwen, a descendant of King Ethelred the Unready. Her husband, John Christian, added his wife's name to his own. He was an enlightened MP inaugurating some effective agricultural reforms, and the patron of several young painters including Romney. The house is not open to the public but the island can be visited by request from Bowness pier.

spent the boyhood holidays he was to recall so vividly in his books for children, and continues close to the shore of the lake. It is a beautiful drive shaded by oak and beech woodlands where there are several delightful car parks, picnic places and nature trails. You pass Peel Island, now owned by the National Trust. Readers of Arthur Ransome will recognise it as 'Wild Cat Island' in *Swallows and Amazons*. Landing is permitted and 'the hidden harbour' waits to be discovered. There are splendid views of the Lakeland peaks to the north and west of Coniston Water as the road follows the lakeshore. But for the best view of Coniston's own mountain, Old Man, visit Brantwood, where John Ruskin lived from 1871 to 1900. His house is to the right of the road and is open to the public.

As you approach the head of the lake, a road joins on the right signposted to Hawkshead. Ignore this and bear left round the head of the lake to meet the B5285. Turn right, following the sign for 'Windermere via ferry', in the direction of Hawkshead. The road winds uphill past a pleasant car park and picnic place at High Cross before meeting the B5285 just north of Hawkshead village. **Turn**

right along the B5285 signed 'Windermere via ferry' and follow the road as it bypasses the village. There are clearly signed car parks if you wish to visit this picturesque village.

The B5285 turns left, again signed 'Windermere via ferry', then right, to run along the shore of Esthwaite Water through gentle green countryside to Near Sawrey. Here you can visit Hill Top, Beatrix Potter's lakeland retreat and the setting for many of her stories. The car park is on the right as you leave the village, beside the Tower Bank Arms which is adjacent to Hill Top.

Continue through Far

Sawrey to the ferry terminal and take the ferry over Windermere. Close on the left is Belle Isle, the largest island on Windermere. The circular, domed house was built in 1774 for a wealthy merchant, Thomas English. **Follow the B5285 to meet the A592. Turn right then almost immediately left, still on the B5285, to meet the A5074. Turn left then almost immediately right, to take the B5284 signed for Crook and Kendal. The road continues through Crook to meet the A591 at a round-about. Continue along the A5284 which brings you back to Kendal.** ■

Sizergh Castle

ULLSWATER, THE LOWTHER VALLEY AND SHAP ABBEY

52 MILES – 3 HOURS
START AND FINISH AT PENRITH

Many people consider Ullswater to be the most beautiful of the Cumbrian lakes. From Pooley Bridge the lake winds south for 7 miles. It is bordered by steep-sided, wooded fells and gradually rises to the great peaks of the High Street Range and Helvellyn. This tour follows the lake's quiet eastern shore past tiny rocky bays shaded with hazel, oak, ash and alder before visiting the pastoral Lowther valley and the limestone scars around Shap.

Leave Penrith heading south along the A6. At the A66 roundabout keep on along the A6 signed for Shap. Cross the medieval bridge over the River Eamont. Drive through Eamont Bridge and turn right along the B5320 signed for Ullswater. On the corner, in a field to the left of the road, is a circular embankment known as King Arthur's Round Table probably dating from 1,000 BC. A few yards further on a sign points right, down a turning to Mayburgh Henge, a huge embankment enclosing a standing stone.

Continue along the B5320 through Tirril. **After a further ³/₄ mile, make a detour down the lane on the right signposted to Barton church.** Park beside the lane to see this astonishing 'minster' church. Once serving a wide area, the church has a magnificent central Norman tower. **Return to the B5320 and turn right to continue to Pooley Bridge at the head of Ullswater.** Car parks give access to the waterside. The pier for the Ullswater steamers, *Raven* and *Lady of the Lake* is opposite the village. If you would like a steamer trip, cross the bridge and follow the B5320 to the pier.

To continue the tour retrace the route along the B5320 to the church in Pooley Bridge. Just past the church turn right A signposted to Howtown and Martindale. At the crossroads turn right, again following the same sign, to take the minor road that traces Ullswater's eastern shore. Hallin Fell rises ahead as this beautiful drive approaches Howtown, a stopping place for the steamers. The road climbs inland to the foot of Martindale, one of Lakeland's most remote valleys and the home of wild red deer. **At the fork take the right-hand**

• PLACES OF INTEREST •

Penrith
Situated on the main route from England to Scotland, Penrith was built to be a refuge. Its narrow roads lead to open areas where animals could be herded for safety. In the ninth and tenth centuries it was the capital of the old kingdom of Cumbria. After the disastrous Scots raid in 1345 a castle was built in the town, but only the curtain wall remains today.

The Church of St Andrew dates from the twelfth century. Interesting old houses cluster around the churchyard. One of them is believed to have been Dame Birkett's infant school attended by Wordsworth, his sister Dorothy, and future wife Mary Hutchinson. At the age of five he climbed Penrith Beacon hill, north of the town, an event he recalls in *The Prelude*.

Penrith Museum is set in a girls' charity school and tells the story of Penrith and the Eden valley. Opening times vary. Telephone: Penrith (01768) 64671.

The Steam Museum is a working museum with steam traction engines, vintage farm machinery, blacksmith's forge and pattern shop, as well as a furnished Victorian cottage. Telephone: (01768) 62154.

Lowther
Lowther Castle is a spectacular ruin, the remains of a mansion built in 1806 to 1811 for the Earl of Lonsdale.

There are two villages on the estate, Lowther Newtown dating from the seventeenth century, and Lowther Village designed by the Adams brothers.

In August the famous Lowther Horse Trials and Country Fair are held in the grounds where there is also a wildlife park, an outdoor activity centre and museum.

For the wildlife park telephone: Hackthorpe (019312) 523.

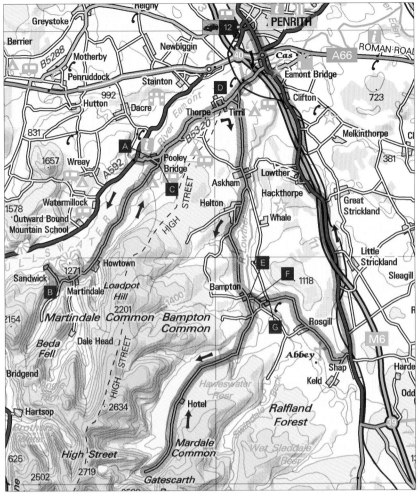

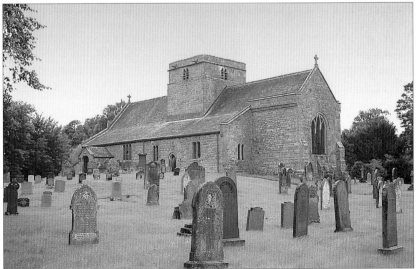

Barton's 'minster' church

Shap Abbey

The only part of the abbey left standing is the great sixteenth-century west tower of the church, but enough remains of the bases of

the other walls to give an idea of its shape and size. Some thirteenth-century buildings survive to first floor level and there is some fine fourteenth-century vaulting.

The abbey was founded by the Canons of the Premonstratensian Order in 1180 – the only abbey in Westmorland – and was the last to be dissolved by Henry VIII in 1540. This reprieve was probably due to its usefulness as a shelter for travellers crossing the inhospitable Shap fells. Much of the stone was carted away to build Lowther Castle.

English Heritage, who maintain the site, provide a helpful map.

Clifton

In the winter of 1745 Bonnie Prince Charlie and his Scottish Jacobites captured Carlisle and advanced south as far as Derby. They were forced to retreat in the snow across the Shap fells along the route of the present A6 by the Duke of Cumberland and his army. Eventually the Scots turned to fight, taking up their positions behind the walls and hedges south of Clifton village at Town End. The result was indecisive.

You can see the 'Rebel Tree', an old oak at Town End Farm, under which five Highlanders were buried. A plaque reads:

Here is buried the men of the Army of Prince Charles who fell at Clifton Moor 18 December, 1745.

The English dead were buried in the churchyard and they are commemorated by a stone.

---

road signposted to Sandwick. **Cross Howegrain Beck and then bear left to the foot of Boredale. Take the joining road on the right** B **for Sandwick.** The road ends by a group of cottages where there is room to park. A footpath leads to Sandwick Bay, an ideal place for a picnic and the start of delightful lakeside walks.

Retrace the route to Pooley Bridge but, at the crossroads just east of the village C**, continue straight on following the sign for Tirril and Yanworth. At the B5320 bear right and retrace the route through Tirril,**

which is on the line of the Roman road, High Street. The Romans built High Street on the route of an old British track to connect Galava, their fort near Ambleside, with that at Brocavum near Penrith. **After about ¼ mile turn right** D **down the minor road signposted to Askham and Haweswater. At the T-junction turn right for Askham.** As you drive south the limestone fells give way to the lush green of the Lowther valley and, if you look left after about 2 miles, you will have a splendid view of the shell of Lowther Castle white against a darkly-wooded hillside.

Drive through Askham, an enchanting village of mainly eighteenth-century houses set either side of a long tree-shaded green. A pleasant break can be made here. There are some lovely walks to the riverside past Askham Hall (private residence of the Earl of Lonsdale) and across the bridge to follow rights-of-way in the grounds of Lowther Castle, which is not open to the public.

Continue through Askham, heading south for Helton. The undulating country is chequered by dry-stone walls reminiscent of the Yorkshire Dales. Limestone scars top the hills east of the river. **Drive through Helton still heading south for Bampton.**

Boats can be hired at Pooley Bridge on Ullswater

Turn right to cross the bridge in Bampton E signposted to Haweswater and Mardale. Keep on, ignoring all side roads, for Haweswater. In a little more than 1 mile, just after a lane leads right at a fork for Burnbanks, the road runs past a cluster of houses at Naddle Gate. There is room to park here. Walk down the road a few yards further to a footpath on the left beside Haweswater Beck which leads the short distance to a waterfall, Thornthwaite Force.

From Naddle Gate the road bears right to trace the eastern shore of Haweswater Reservoir. In 1940 Manchester Water Corporation flooded the valley, increasing the length of Haweswater from 2½ to 4 miles. A dam, 120 feet (37 m) high was built, and the village of Mardale drowned. The shores of the reservoir may appear bleak and lonely after the graceful beauty of Ullswater, but the whole area is a marvellous place for wildlife. The road runs through Naddle Woods, scheduled as a Site of Special Scientific Interest on account of its rare lichens and mosses. It is a good idea to have binoculars to hand as golden eagles have been re-introduced

and red deer may be spotted on the fells.

The road beside Haweswater runs along steep-sided fells reminiscent of Wast Water to a car park. From here there is a fine view north-west over the water to the massive crags of the High Street range. Two tarns are cradled in the foothills. The approach to both is through the gate at the end of the road. Continue for 50 yards (46 m) to a signpost.

There are two options here. You can keep ahead following the sign for Kentmere for ¾ mile to reach Small Water, or turn right to cross a stream, then left for 1 mile to climb to Blea Water. This tarn is 207 feet (63 m) in depth, the deepest in the Lake District.

Retrace the route to Bampton. Just over the bridge turn right F for Bampton Grange. Bear left to cross the sandstone bridge over the River Lowther G and drive through the village following the sign for Shap. Ignore all side roads as the route heads west, then turns south down the eastern side of the Lowther valley.

About 1 mile after the turning on the right for Rosgill, look right over an iron gate to see a group of prehistoric standing stones, the remains of a circle which includes the well known Thunder Stone. **Shortly after, a lane is signposted on the right for the ruins of Shap Abbey. Turn right here to follow a narrow lane which dips down to a large car park beside the ruins.**

Retrace the route back to the road and head east to meet the A6 in Shap village. Turn left for Penrith. The A6 follows the old north-south route over the high fells on the course of a turnpike road built in 1763 to connect Kendal and Eamont Bridge. The road crosses the motorway several times as it approaches Clifton village, the site of the last pitched battle fought in England. Clifton Hall, a three-storey peel tower, stands on the left of the road at the north end of the village. Dating from the fifteenth century, the tower is intact and open for exploration every day throughout the year. **The A6 continues to the A66 roundabout and from there takes you to the centre of Penrith.** ∎

THE EDEN VALLEY, INGLEWOOD AND THE WESTERN SHORE OF ULLSWATER

48 MILES – 2 HOURS
START AND FINISH AT PENRITH

North and east of Penrith the River Eden runs through a tranquil valley dotted with attractive red sandstone villages. Settlements have been made here from earliest times, and this tour follows the valley to the second largest prehistoric stone circle in England known as Long Meg and her Daughters. This fertile countryside on the borders of the Lake District fells has always attracted wealthy families and visits are made to the great houses at Hutton-in-the-Forest and Dalemain. The return route follows the beautiful western shore of Ullswater.

Leave Penrith along the A6 heading north. Drive through Townhead and at the foot of Fair Hill turn right A for Langwathby. After ¼ mile the road forks. Take the right-hand road for Langwathby. The steep, wooded slopes of Beacon Hill rise on the left. There is still a building on the top – the Pike – from which a warning beacon could be lit. The beacon flared for the last time in earnest in 1745 when Bonnie Prince

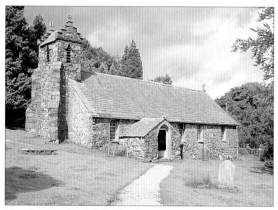

Matterdale church built by local craftsmen

Charlie marched on Penrith.

At the junction with the A686 bear left B and shortly after, when the road divides, leave the A686 and take the right-hand road for Edenhall. You will see the iron gates of the entrance to Eden Hall ahead. Only the coach-house remains of the great mansion that once stood here, the home of the Musgrave family from 1500 to 1900. The famous 'Luck of Eden Hall' is a medieval glass goblet in a

fifteenth-century leather case, said to have been a gift of the fairies who left the message 'If the cup should break or fall farewell to luck of Edenhall'. The goblet is now in the the Victoria and Albert Museum.

In front of the gates the road bears left to run through the village. After Edenhall the road bears left and continues north to meet the A686. Turn right to cross the bridge over the River Eden to Langwathby. The village is a station on the famous Leeds-Settle-Carlisle line which runs the whole length of the Eden valley. **In the village turn left for Little Salkeld C.** The road now follows the east side of the river and goes under the railway. **Keep straight on for Little Salkeld. Cross Briggle Beck.** Just over the bridge on the right is Little Salkeld's early eighteenth-century working water-mill. It is open to the public and tours of the mill are arranged.

The road turns right in Little Salkeld. Follow the

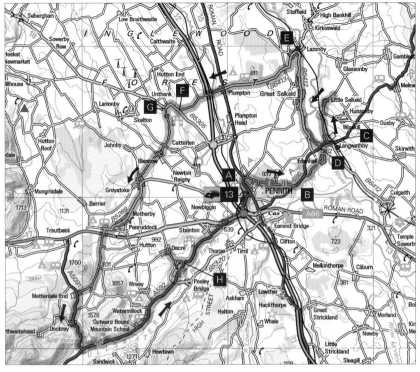

signs for Long Meg and her Daughters. A signposted track leads left from the road to this magnificent circle nearly 400 feet (122 m) in diameter, comprising approximately 59 stones. Try counting them – it is said that if you come up with the same number twice they will all come to life! To one side stands the tallest stone, Long Meg herself,

nearly 18 feet (5.5 m) high. She commands a splendid view over almost the whole extent of the Eden valley west to the Lake District fells and east to the great sweep of the Pennine hills.

Across the river is Great Salkeld, the next village on the route. A flood in the fourteenth century swept away the bridge between the two villages and no

one has got round to building another one!

So, retrace the route to Langwathby, turning right in the village to cross the Eden along the A686. At the next crossroads (possibly unsignposted) turn right D to follow the B6412 north along the west bank of the river to Great Salkeld. In this

---

• PLACES OF INTEREST •

Little Salkeld Mill
The present mill is the third to have been built on the site. Water from the beck turns two 'overshot' wheels, the larger one drives the millstones and the sack hoist and the other powers the machinery which cleans the grain.

The mill shop sells freshly-milled flour as well as bread and cakes and there is a tearoom. An exhibition about the mill is displayed.

The shop is open weekdays throughout the year 10.30–5. Tours of the mill throughout the

day, Monday, Tuesday and Thursday. Telephone: Langwathby (0176881) 523.

Long Meg and her Daughters
Long Meg is inscribed with faint 'cup and ring' markings which can be seen elsewhere on northern standing stones. Her four corners face the four points of the compass. The rays of the setting midwinter sun fall across her dividing the circle exactly in half. But whether the circle was an astronomical device or had some religious or other use remains a

mystery. According to legend Long Meg was a witch who used to dance on the Sabbath with her daughters when she should have been attending church. For this sin they were all turned into stone. Wordsworth saw the circle late in life and wrote in a letter 'Everybody has heard of it, and so had I from early childhood, but had never seen it before. Next to Stonehenge, it is beyond dispute the most notable relic of the kind that this or any other country contains.' Long Meg also inspired a sonnet.

The beautiful view from the seat outside Matterdale church

picturesque village the church is dedicated to St Cuthbert on the site where his body is said to have rested. The church has a fourteenth-century peel tower which was a place of refuge during Scottish raids, and a triple-arched Norman doorway.

Continue north along the B6412 to meet the B6413 in Lazonby. This village is also a station on the Leeds-Settle-Carlisle line. **The route turns left here E along the B6413 for Plumpton to leave the Eden valley. But first turn right in Lazonby to drive the short distance to the river.** This is crossed by a splendid sandstone bridge dated 1762.

Return to E and continue through the village, past a joining road on the right, to bear left along the B6413. After a sharp bend go straight over the next crossroads. The road runs over low fells to Plumpton. Keep straight on over the A6 following the sign for Hutton-in-the-Forest and Unthank to cross the River Petteril. You will enter the once densely-wooded area of

---

• PLACES OF INTEREST •

Hutton-in-the-Forest
Throughout the fourteenth and fifteenth centuries the Scots made frequent raids through what was then the Royal Forest of Inglewood. The number of defensive peel towers north and west of Penrith bears witness to these raids. The Hutton family built the massive peel tower and, three hundred years later, the castle was enlarged by the Fletchers, wealthy merchants from Cockermouth. It is now the home of Lord and Lady Inglewood.

Inside the house there is a splendidly-panelled gallery with carved oak furniture and a collection of tapestries, paintings, china and armour. Teas are served in the house.

The grounds are planted with many fine specimen trees and there is a woodland nature walk. The grounds and gardens are open all year, Sunday–Friday 11–5 and the house Wednesday–Saturday 1–4. Telephone: Skelton (017684) 84449.

Dalemain
There has been a settlement on this site since Saxon times, and today the house reflects a wide range of architectural styles. The peel tower dates from the twelfth century. Later a hall was added converting the building into a manor house. The two wings were built during the reign of Elizabeth I and the facade of pink sandstone ashlar was completed in 1750. Inside there are grand oak-panelled rooms, a maze of winding passages and unexpected corners, including a priest's hole which is behind the store cupboard in the work-room.

Lunches and teas are available in the Medieval Hall. The house and gardens are open 27 March–2 October, daily except Friday and Saturday 11.15–5. Telephone: Pooley Bridge (017684) 86450.

Inglewood Forest and, at one time, the largest royal hunting forest in England. **The road continues over the motorway to meet the B5305. Turn right** **F** **signed Unthank for Hutton-in-the-Forest and bear left to the entrance to this imposing mansion.** Built around a fourteenth-century peel tower, the house was one of the three main manors of the Royal Forest of Inglewood. The house, gardens and surrounding woods are open to the public.

From the house continue past a turning on the right. At the next junction leave the B5305 and turn left **G** **in the direction of Greystoke. Go over the next crossroads, keeping on for Little Blencow. In Little Blencow bear right at the first fork then bear left for Greystoke.** Pass Blencow Hall on the right, a fortified manor with a partly ruined peel tower. **At the T-junction turn left to enter Greystoke.** Pause here if possible. Attractive sandstone houses cluster round a triangular green in the centre of which stands an old stone cross. The large collegiate church is down a lane on the left just past the green. It has beautifully carved misericords and an east window containing medieval stained glass showing the devil being crushed by a saint. Follow the footpath running north from the church for about 100 yards (92 m) to see a plague stone with its scooped-out top to hold the vinegar used to cleanse coins.

Drive through Greystoke heading south along the B5288 for Motherby. After Motherby keep to the B5288 turning right at the T-junction, then left following the sign for Penrith and Matterdale. Cross the A66 and continue down the minor road ahead for Matterdale. The road runs south through this beautiful valley to meet the A5091 at Matterdale End. Turn left for Ullswater.

Just before the next minor road on the left, signposted to Penruddock, is Matterdale church, a gem built by local craftsmen. There is room to park by the churchyard gate.

Beautiful views of Ullswater open ahead as the road descends to meet the A592 which runs along the lakeshore. Turn left for a few yards to the car park on the left. Footpaths lead from here to Aira Force, one of lakeland's most splendid waterfalls, and Gowbarrow Park where the Wordsworths saw the daffodils, immortalized in his poem.

Follow the A592 as it runs along the shores of Ullswater for over 5 miles. There are glorious views all the way. **As you approach the north end of the lake, keep to the A592 as it bears left signed for Dalemain with the River Eamont on the right. In a little under 1 mile turn left** **H** **for Dacre. (The turning may be unsigned.)** As you approach the village there is an

access area with parking on the right just before the bridge. Walk up to the village to visit the Norman church (a few yards up the lane past the post office) built on the site of a Saxon monastery. Dotted around the churchyard are four mysterious stone bears. Looking at each in turn they appear to tell the story of a sleeping bear waking up and eating a cat-like animal. From the churchyard there is a fine view of the restored fourteenth-century peel tower of Dacre Castle.

Return to the A592. Bear left beside the River Eamont and cross Dacre Bridge to the entrance to Dalemain. There is a fascinating mansion concealing an Elizabethan house behind a Georgian facade. The house and grounds are open to the public.

Keep on the A592 following the west bank of the Eamont. When you meet the A66 turn right at the roundabout. At the next intersection turn left along the A592 towards the centre of Penrith. ■

Long Meg with some of her daughters in the background

THE THREE CASTLES TOUR: BROUGHAM, APPLEBY AND BROUGH

65 MILES – 3 HOURS
START AND FINISH AT PENRITH

This is a splendid tour, particularly if you like castles, as it includes three of the finest in Cumbria. They were all restored by the redoubtable Lady Anne Clifford in the seventeenth century in defiance of Cromwell. Today Brougham and Brough are ruins but Appleby, Lady Anne's favourite castle, is a family home and the keep is open to the public. The tour also contains a rich variety of scenery. The fertile meadows beside the River Eden and the wooded banks of the River Lyvennet contrast with the wild moorland of the Pennine foothills.

Leave Penrith heading south along the A6. At the A66 roundabout keep straight on to cross the River Eamont and pass the junction with the B5320 on the right. The A6 curves left to cross the River Lowther. Immediately after crossing, bear left along the B6262. On the right, enclosed by a massive wall, is Brougham Hall. Built on the site of a Roman fort, the hall was once known as the Windsor of the North and was one of the homes of the Lord Chancellor. Restored in 1985, it is now a local crafts centre and welcomes visitors.

At the next crossroads turn left following the sign for Brougham Castle. A footpath leads left to the castle opposite a car park on the right. The ruins are dominated by the great moated Norman keep and are magnificently sited overlooking the River Eamont.

Return to the crossroads and keep straight on A down Moon Lane. The road bends right to a T-junction at High Dykes. Turn left here in the direction of Cliburn. Just before the road crosses the railway, you will see Wetheriggs Pottery on the right. This is a working Victorian country pottery complete with nineteenth-century steam engine and machinery. Visitors are welcome.

Ignore all side roads and continue to the crossroads in the centre of Cliburn. Turn right to cross the river and head south for Morland. Bear left into Morland village following the sign for Bolton. There is room to park on the left of the road, opposite the pub. Morland must be everyone's idea

of a charming English village with deep-eaved cottages on either side of a beck crossed by tiny footbridges, two ancient inns, and a Saxon church tower.

To continue the tour leave the pub on your right, cross the bridge and follow the road as it bears right. Keep on to cross the River Lyvennet to a T-junction and turn left. At the next T-junction turn right signposted to Bolton. Continue to drive into Bolton. This is a small village on the west side of the River Eden. The church has a Norman nave and

Brougham Castle

doorways. The northern doorway is surmounted by a medieval carving of knights jousting.

Turn right in Bolton B to follow the Eden valley south-east for Colby. The road runs through Colby, then bears left and crosses Colby Beck to meet the B6260 opposite the castle in Appleby-in-Westmorland. The entrance to the castle overlooks the top end of Appleby's attractive main street. Standing high above the River Eden, the keep of the castle offers a magnificent view of the Pennine hills.

Turn left C past the castle and keep to the B6260 as it curves right and crosses the Eden to meet the B6542. Turn right along the B6542 signed for Brough. Follow the signs for Brough to join the A66 and continue south-west in the direction of Brough. On the right the River Eden winds lazily through green meadows, but south and east rise the

Appleby's main street, Boroughgate, slopes downhill from the castle. Tall black and white pillars stand at either end, and are known as High Cross and Low Cross.

rounded slopes of the Pennines. **After 2 miles turn right D along the B6259 signposted to Sandford and Warcop. At the Y-junction, just past the dismantled railway, bear left, still along the B6259 which dips to the east bank of the Eden before running beside woods into Warcop village. Keep to the B6259 as**

it bears right round this delightfully unspoilt village and continues south up the Eden valley. Look out for the maypole in Warcop village.

After about 1¹/₄ miles the road crosses the dismantled railway. Leave the B6259 and continue straight on for Great Musgrave. The name is deceptive as this is a tiny village but very

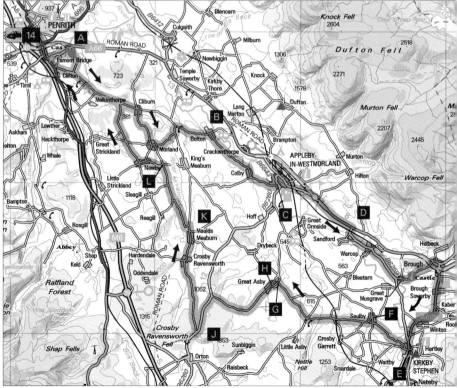

SCALE 1:250 000 OR 1 INCH TO 4 MILES *1 CM TO 2.5 KM*

Brougham Castle

The ruins of the castle stand in the north-west corner of a Roman fort, Brocavum, meaning 'the hill of the badgers'. As most of the stone was used to build the castle, only the foundations of the fort remain. The earliest part of the castle, the keep, dates from the late twelfth century. Its purpose was to protect the intersection of the main route to the north with the important route leading west from York.

Towards the end of the thirteenth century the castle passed by marriage to the Cliffords who added inner and outer gatehouses. Although Lady Anne Clifford restored the castle after its slighting in the Civil War by Cromwell, it is now only an impressive ruin. However, it is still possible to recapture some of the castle's former glory.

The castle is open 1 April–30 September daily 10–6. Rest of year Wednesday–Sunday 10–4. Telephone: Penrith (01768) 62488.

Wetheriggs Pottery

The pottery has a licensed restaurant and a coffee shop. Open daily 10–6. Telephone: (01768) 62946.

Appleby-in-Westmorland

Appleby was formerly the County town of Westmorland. Sited in a loop of the River Eden it still has the atmosphere of a medieval market town protected by its superb castle.

The castle is of the motte-and-bailey type and dates from the twelfth century. After its restoration by Lady Anne Clifford it has remained a private residence, but the keep with its impressive great hall is open to visitors. A conservation centre in the grounds is home for rare breeds of British farm animals and unusual birds. Open 26 March–31 October daily 10–5. Telephone: Appleby (017683) 51402.

The Appleby Horse Fair is held on the second Wednesday in June.

Brough

This small town has been a settlement for almost two thousand years. Throughout the nineteenth century it was an important coaching town and is famous today for its horse fair held at the end of September. St Michael's Church is mainly thirteenth- and fifteenth-century.

The ruins of the castle are sited on a steep moorland escarpment above the south bank of the Swindale Beck. It stands in the north-east corner of the Roman Fort of Veteris which was built to guard the passes of Stainmore and Mallerstang where their road continued to Kirkby Thore. The castle probably began as a defensive triangular enclosure late in the eleventh century. Additions were made in later centuries and, after a fire in the sixteenth century, it was restored by Lady Anne Clifford who added the cylindrical tower in the south-east corner which is named Clifford's tower after her. Open 1 April–30 September daily 10–6. Rest of year Wednesday–Sunday 10–4.

Crosby Ravensworth

The name of this picturesque village suggests a Viking settlement, but many generations have left their mark in this secluded spot beside the Lyvennet. Footpaths lead past the church to a large prehistoric enclosure. There is the line of a Roman road to the south-west and the shaft of a seventh-century cross, used as a centre for worshippers before the church was built, stands in the churchyard.

The twelfth-century keep of Appleby Castle, known as Caesar's Tower, surrounded by part of the castle's curtain wall

attractive. **Leave the village and at the Y-junction take the right-hand road (Musgrave Lane).** This turns a little south to run along the north bank of the Swindale Beck towards Brough, a small market town nestling at the foot of Stainmore Fell. **The road crosses the A66 and runs to meet the B6276. Turn right signed for Brough to drive into Market Brough. Take the next road on the right, the A685, signed for Keswick and Kirkby Stephen. The road runs under the A66 and, a few yards further on, you will see a sign on the right for Brough Castle. Turn right along the lane to the car park near the castle entrance.**

Return to the A685 and turn right signed for Kendal. Keep to the A685 as it runs south to approach Kirkby Stephen. This historic town is beautifully situated beside the River Eden close to its source in the High Seat fells. There is ample parking if you wish to explore on foot.

Drive through Kirkby Stephen, pass the junction with the B6259 on the right and take the road on the right E opposite the church, signed for Soulby. Shortly after, the road bears right to cross Scandal Beck and right again to the crossroads in Soulby. **Turn left F, signposted to Great Asby, to take the moorland road running west. At the cross-**

roads bear right for Great Asby. At the T-junction turn left **G**. Drive through this attractive village sheltered by high fells threaded by streams. Great Asby is a marvellous centre for walks. There is roadside parking in the village and several footpaths lead to perfect waterside picnic spots.

In the centre of Great Asby the road turns right over a bridge with a church on the right. Turn left **H** and continue along Sayle Lane following the sign for Orton.

Follow Sayle Lane as it crosses the moors and bears right over craggy fells. Over a cattle-grid the road becomes unfenced and runs over open moorland to meet the B6260. Turn left in the direction of Orton, but before reaching the village take the road on the right just before a cattle-grid **J** signposted to Crosby Ravensworth.

The road now runs north along the east side of the lovely valley of the River Lyvennet. This fertile valley has been settled since the Bronze Age and on the surrounding fells there are over ninety sites of prehistoric villages. **The road crosses the river at Holme Bridge and continues through Crosby Ravensworth bearing right past the church and heading north beside the river.**

Drive through Maulds Meaburn and follow the riverside. Just past Meaburn Hall turn left **K before the bridge following the sign for Morland and Penrith. Shortly after, the road turns sharply right for 1 mile, then left for a few yards, before bearing** right to resume a northerly heading for Morland and Penrith. Pass the turning for Sleagill and take the turning on the left **L** signposted to Newby.

Continue through Newby following the sign for Great Strickland and Shap, then turn right following the sign for Great Strickland and Penrith. Continue straight over the crossroads following the sign for Cliburn and Penrith. At the T-junction turn left for Penrith and continue past Wetheriggs Pottery to meet the A6 at Clifton Cross. Turn right along the A6 and follow the main road over Lowther Bridge and Eamont Bridge to the A66 roundabout. Keep straight on along the A6 for the centre of Penrith. ■

Brough Castle

THE RIVER GRETA, CASTLERIGG STONE CIRCLE AND THIRLMERE'S WESTERN SHORE

60 MILES – 2½ HOURS
START AND FINISH AT KESWICK

Some of the best-loved scenes in the Lake District can be enjoyed on this comprehensive tour from Keswick, one of the most beautifully situated of all Lakeland towns. The route follows the shores of six lakes, including the quieter western shore of Thirlmere with its waterside picnic places and nature trails. Early in the tour visits are made to the prehistoric stone circle at Castlerigg and the interesting village of Dacre. The route crosses Kirkstone Pass, the highest in the Lake District, so beware early snowfalls.

Leave Keswick along the A5271 heading east along the south bank of the River Greta. After you have crossed the disused rail track, the small bridge you will see on the left is named after Raisley Calvert. He lent Windebrowe House which stands east of the bridge (now a riding school run by the Calvert Trust Centre for the Disabled) to William and Dorothy Wordsworth in the spring of 1794. He was cared for by William during his last illness, and in gratitude left William a legacy which enabled him to set up home with Dorothy and devote all his time to writing.

Continue for about ¼ mile, pass the junction with the A591, and take the next minor road on the right  signed for Castlerigg Stone Circle. There is parking beside the road on the left opposite the footpath to the circle.

Continue to a T-junction and turn left for a few yards to another T-junction. Turn right and follow the road as it loops round to meet the A66.

Turn right to follow the A66 for just a few yards, then take the minor road on the left **B** signposted to Threlkeld. At the T-junction in the village turn left to a car park. Threlkeld lies on the lower slopes of Blencathra, and from the car park a short walk beside Blease Gill leads to a waterfall.

Return to the village centre and bear left past the church to follow the road as it curves right to meet the A66. Turn left and follow the A66 for about 7 miles. Leave the A66 and turn right down a minor road signposted to Dacre **C**. After about ¾ mile you will see the church and castle in this historic village ahead, a little to the left of the road. Just before entering the village there is roadside parking. Walk into Dacre and turn left past the post office to visit the church. From the churchyard there is a good view of Dacre Castle with its splendid peel tower.

From Dacre continue south

Looking across Ullswater to the mountains of the High Street Range

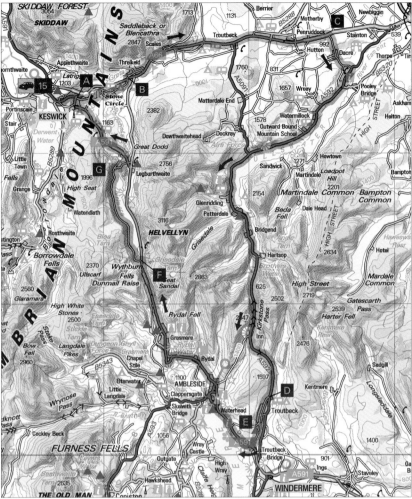

to cross Dacre Beck and meet the A592. **Turn right along the main road which runs down to a T-junction on the northern shore of Ullswater. Turn right, keeping to the A592.** The road traces the lakeshore giving glorious views of Helvellyn and the steadily rising wall of the High Street range. After about 5 miles a car park on the right gives access to Aira Force, a magnificent series of falls. For a wonderful view of the lake, take the footpath leading right from the path to the falls which climbs the steep side of Gowbarrow to a seat on the top of Yew Crag – about 1½ miles round.

Keep along the A592 as it runs through Glenridding and Patterdale and climbs to Brothers Water. A car park just before this small lake gives access to the shore, a favourite spot for birdwatchers. **The road continues over Kirkstone Pass, which although high, does not offer any real difficulties to the motorist.** Bleak crags lie either side, but from the highest point, near the inn, there is a marvellous view over the southern fells. **Ignore the first minor road on the right which is just past the inn. Take the next road on the right** D **signposted to Ambleside to drive through the old-world village of Troutbeck.** Many houses have open spinning galleries – a

reminder of the importance of wool to cottage economy in the past – and typical lakeland barns built into the hillsides. After about 1 mile, just before a junction with a minor road, you will see Town End, a remarkable survival of a yeoman farmer's house, dating from the beginning of the seventeenth century, on the right. **To visit the house, which is open to the public, do not take the left-hand road at the junction, but continue along the minor road for a few yards. The car park for Town End is down the first entry on the right.**

From the car park return to the junction and turn sharply right E to continue down the

Keswick

Keswick is magnificently sited at the foot of the rounded slopes of Skiddaw, overlooking Derwent Water and the Borrowdale fells. It is an attractive town with intriguing narrow streets and old grey stone buildings. In the centre of the market-place stands the nineteenth-century Moot Hall, now the information centre. There is an excellent railway museum, and the Fitz Park Museum contains a collection of manuscripts by Southey, Wordsworth, Walpole and Ruskin. Southey lived for forty years at Greta Hall, which is now part of Lairthwaite school, and cared for Coleridge and his family. Crosthwaite church, north-west of the town, has a memorial to Southey. The church is the oldest structure in the valley, dating from 1553. A unique attraction in Keswick is the pencil museum in the Cumberland Pencil Factory. The first pencils in the world were made using graphite mined from the Borrowdale fells.

Launches leave from the boat landings at Lake Shore. They depart every half hour and the circuit of the lake takes about fifty minutes. There are stops at six jetties around the lake: Ashness Bridge, Lodore Falls, High Brandelhow, Low Brandelhow, Hawes End and Nicol End. You can board or leave at any of these stages, and they make ideal starting points for walks. Boats can also be hired from Lake Shore.

Threlkeld

The village is close to the site of a Romano-British settlement, occupied from the third to the eighth century. The Celtic tradition is also recalled by the names of the mountain, Blencathra, and the nearby river, Glenderamackin.

---

valley to meet the A591. Turn right for Ambleside along the eastern shore of Windermere. You pass Brockhole Visitor Centre on the left – a beautiful Edwardian house offering a perfect introduction to Lakeland.

At Waterhead leave the A591 and bear left following the sign for Keswick, Coniston and the Langdales. Keep on following the sign for Keswick, taking the one-way system through Ambleside to meet the A591 at a T-junction. Turn left past quaint Bridge House (now a National Trust Information Centre). If you wish to stop in Ambleside the entrance to a large car park is shortly on the left.

To continue the tour head north along the A591 along the valley of the River Rothay. On the left rise the wooded slopes of Loughrigg Fell with a narrow road curving along its

Early morning sunlight on Castlerigg Stone Circle in its lonely moorland setting

foot. This was one of Dorothy Wordsworth's favourite walks when collecting mail from Ambleside or visiting her friends. The valley was also a favourite with other literary figures including Matthew Arnold, whose father, Dr Arnold of Rugby, built Fox How beside the River Rothay.

The road runs close to the river as it approaches Rydal. Here a sign indicates a turning on the right to Rydal Mount, Wordsworth's last lakeland home. It is open to visitors. The road hugs the northern shore of Rydal Water and leads to car parks and picnic places at White Moss. It then curves round Baneriggs to reveal Grasmere surrounded by its wooded fells.

Follow the road along the lakeshore to a lane on the right, signposted to Dove Cottage. It was here that William and Dorothy Wordsworth made their first home in the Lake District and where he wrote some

Keswick across Derwent Water

of his finest poetry. The road opposite leads to Grasmere village where the poet is buried.

Continue the tour along the A591 as it climbs up Dunmail Raise. This is the traditional dividing line between north and south Lakeland. This gloomy expanse of moorland was the site of a battle between the Norse King Dunmail of Cumbria and the Saxon King Edmund. Dunmail lost, and a cairn at the top of the pass is reputed to be over his burial place, but legend has it that Dunmail escaped over Helvellyn, discarding his treasure in Grisedale Tarn on the way.

The road drops to the head of pine-fringed Thirlmere, now a reservoir. In 1890 Manchester Corporation Waterworks built a dam across the north end of the lake, raising the water level by 54 feet (16.4 m). Wythburn village vanished beneath the water and almost five hundred acres of farmland were flooded. Only the church survived on the opposite side of the water.

As you approach Thirlmere turn left **F** **following the sign for Armboth.** This village has also disappeared under the lake. **Cross the Wythburn Beck.** There is a pleasant waterside car park here. **Follow the minor road that runs along the western shore of Thirlmere.** There are views over the lake to the rounded slopes of Helvellyn.

Nearing the north end of the lake the road divides **G**. **Keep straight on (left-hand road) for Keswick. The road curves right to meet the A591. Turn left for Keswick along the A591 to cross St John's Beck with the jagged outcrops of High Rigg on the right. The road bears north over moorland. Continue for about 4 miles to meet the A5271. Turn left to return along the south bank of the River Greta to Keswick.** ■

• PLACES OF INTEREST •

Castlerigg Stone Circle
This prehistoric stone circle is between three and four thousand years old, older than Stonehenge. It stands in an appropriate setting in a natural amphitheatre surrounded by bleak fells. Thirty-eight stones are set in an oval with a further ten stones forming an inner rectangle.

As with all stone circles, only guesses can be made as to its use, but even today the sight of these mighty stones is awe-inspiring. They made a deep impression on John Keats who walked to see them one very wet November evening. In *Hyperion 2* he recalls his visit to the *dismal cirque of Druid stones, upon a forlorn moor*.

Dacre
The church is Norman, but it possibly stands on the site of an Anglo-Saxon monastery described by St Bede. North of the church excavations have revealed a

Christian cemetery containing ninth-century coins and to the south an eighth-century stylus or pen has been discovered in a stone-lined drain. The churchyard contains four stone bears, uniquely carved and impossible to date, fragments of an eighth-century Anglian cross and a Viking cross dating from the tenth century.

Town End
Open 1 April–30 October
Tuesday–Friday and Sunday 1–5.
Telelephone: Ambleside
(015394) 32628.

Rydal Mount
Open March–October daily
9.30–5. November–February
Wednesday–Monday 10–4.
Telephone: (015394) 33002.

Dove Cottage
Open daily 9.30–5.30. Closed
10 January–6 February.
Telephone: (015394) 35544.

CRUMMOCK WATER, BUTTERMERE AND BORROWDALE

42 MILES – 1½ HOURS
START AND FINISH AT KESWICK

This is a short tour, but one you will wish to take slowly as the scenery is spectacular. The route climbs over the Whinlatter Pass to run beside Crummock Water and Buttermere. It then crosses Honister Hause into Borrowdale, thought by many to be the most beautiful of the lakeland valleys. To return to Keswick the route traces the lovely eastern shore of Derwent Water. The detour from the shore to Watendlath should be avoided at busy times as the road is very narrow with a limited number of passing places.

Leave Keswick along the A5271 heading north-west in the direction of Great Crosthwaite. The road crosses the River Derwent and follows its west bank. **When the road turns right 🅰 keep ahead along the B5289, which bears left to cross Derwent Bridge and meet the A66. Bear left along the A66 for a little more than 1 mile, then leave the main road and turn left along the B5292 for Braithwaite.**

This is a quiet village at the foot of Whinlatter Pass. **Drive straight over the crossroads in the village, keeping to the B5292 signed for Whinlatter which bears right to climb through Thornthwaite Woods.** You pass a car park on the left, then shortly after, another car park and picnic place at Noble Knott. Stop here for a magnificent view over the southern end of Bassenthwaite Lake to the western slopes of Skiddaw. Waymarked forest trails

also leave from here.

The road dips and then climbs past two more car parks and picnic areas to the Forestry Commission's interesting Whinlatter Forest Visitor Centre. Waymarked forest trails with view indicators can be followed from the centre.

Past the sheer face of Whinlatter Crag the road descends Lorton fells to a car park on the right by Scawgill Bridge. From here you can take

A mountain beck at the foot of Honister Pass

the signed Spout Force walk (3 miles round) to see the waterfall. There is a short cut to the waterfall which is also indicated (2 miles round).

Follow the road down into Lorton Vale, a fertile valley threaded by the River Cocker, to High Lorton. Behind the village hall, known as Yew Tree Hall, stands the famous yew tree in whose shade George Fox preached to the villagers in spite of the presence of Cromwell's soldiers. The event inspired Wordsworth's poem *Yew Trees*.

To see the yew tree, turn left into Lorton village following the sign for Buttermere. At the T-junction turn left. Drive past the inn and take the second turning on the left signed for Boonbeck and Scales. After a few yards there is room to park and turn. The yew tree is directly ahead. Return to the B5292.

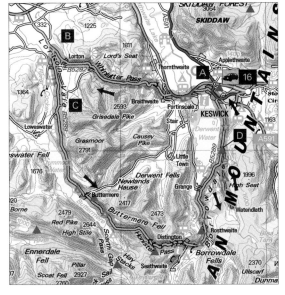

Continue along the B5292 in the direction of Cockermouth to the junction with the B5289. Turn left B along the B5289. Keep to the main road past a sign for Lorton. You pass Low Lorton Hall, a seventeenth-century house adjoining a fifteenth-century peel tower with an interesting history. **Continue south keeping to the B5289. When the road divides turn left C keeping to the B5289 for Buttermere.** Glorious views of Crummock Water open ahead. Melbreak rises to the right of the lake and Grasmoor to the left. To the south, the northern crags of Great Gable and Green Gable are outlined against the sky beyond the Buttermere fells and Fleetwith Pike.

The road follows the eastern shore of Crummock Water where there are two car parks at the foot of Rannerdale. A footpath leads for over 1/2 mile up this secret valley, a cul-de-sac, hidden from the south by Hause Point. It is said that a Norman army under William Rufus was lured by the Viking settlers into the valley, believing it led to a pass, and were massacred. The road continues to Hause Point where there is a car park giving splendid views. Then the road descends to cross Mill Beck into Buttermere village, a small settlement sheltered by high fells on the narrow strip of land between Crummock Water and Buttermere. Perched above the

• *PLACES OF INTEREST* •

Whinlatter Forest Visitor Centre
The centre tells the story of the surrounding Thornthwaite Forest in a variety of ways including an audio-visual presentation and computer games. There is a working model of the forest and an indoor 'conservation' playroom. Tearoom. Open: February–December daily 10–5.30. Closed January. Telephone: Braithwaite (017687) 78469.

A few yards away from the centre are the trees planted by the Forestry Commission in 1919 – the first to be planted anywhere in Britain.

Low Lorton Hall
During the Reformation, this house became a refuge for Roman Catholic priests and its priest's holes and secret escape routes are still there. The house also contains fine oak panelling and Jacobean and Carolingian furniture. It is open by

appointment. Telephone: Lorton (01900) 252.

Buttermere
This small village achieved fame in 1795 when J. Budworth published *A Fortnight's Ramble in the Lakes*. He had stayed at the Fish Inn and met the landlord's fifteen-year-old daughter, 'the Beauty of Buttermere', who had told him a moving story. A stranger had come to the village claiming to be the Honourable Alexander Hope MP. She had married him, but he turned out to be a bigamist wanted for forgery and was hanged a year later. Mary gave birth to a still-born child. Her story touched the hearts of the public and was featured by Coleridge in the *Morning Post* under the heading 'A Romantic Marriage'. However, the 'Beauty of Buttermere' was not left desolate. She later married a local farmer and brought up a large family. She is buried at Caldbeck.

village on a rocky shelf is the tiny church, typical of the Lake District, entered through a wrought iron porch showing a shepherd leading a ewe and a lamb. From the car parks in the village a footpath leads for about 2½ miles around Buttermere. Another footpath leads to Scale Force, the highest waterfall in the Lake District with a single spectacular fall of 172 feet (52 m) and two others of 20 feet (6.1 m). The distance round is about 3½ miles.

Follow the B5289 as it continues close to the eastern shore of Buttermere among magnificent scenery. Just past the point where the Gatesgarthdale Beck flows into the lake, the road crosses the beck, passing a car park on the left. Ahead are the sheer slopes of Fleetwith Pike, and the white cross you will see on one of the ridges was erected in memory of a girl who fell to her death descending the mountain. **The road now begins the climb beside Gatesgarthdale Beck over Honister Pass.** There

is a car park at the top at Honister Hause close to the slate quarries operated by The Buttermere and Westmorland Green Slate Company. A winding descent follows to Seatoller, a hamlet built after the quarries were opened in 1643 to house the workers. The Lake District National Park authorities have established a base here with an information centre providing natural history exhibitions, talks and guided walks.

The road continues past a minor road on the right to Seathwaite, crosses the River Derwent and turns north to Rosthwaite in the centre of the Borrowdale valley. A car park at the north end of the village gives access to several footpaths. A lovely short walk leads to Johnny Wood, one of the beautiful broad-leaved woodlands which were planted in this area to replace the natural forest cleared to supply the iron-ore furnaces.

Keep ahead along the B5289 as it runs beside the River Derwent. It is hemmed in by the sheer sides of Scawdel

in the west and Grange Fell in the east, a narrow way known as The Jaws of Borrowdale. A footpath from the Bowder Stone car park on the right leads to this huge boulder left behind by a glacier at the end of the last Ice Age. Lovely views of Derwent Water are revealed as the road approaches the lake and passes the turning for Grange. About ½ mile past the Swiss Lodore Hotel there is a car park on the left by the waterside, giving access to a footpath leading to the Lodore Waterfall which is behind the hotel.

Follow the road for about another ½ mile, then leave the lakeshore and turn sharp right D up the narrow road with passing places signposted to Watendlath. After a little more than ¼ mile you will see Ashness Bridge and a car park on the right. This is a pack-horse bridge from which there are superb views. Higher up the road there is another car park at Surprise View. Opposite the car park the ground falls away to reveal the whole of Derwent Water. **Continue to Watendlath.**

The Bowder Stone – a 'glacial erratic'

Ashness pack-horse bridge with Derwent Water in the background

There is a small group of greystone farms beside a tarn in a hollow among the hills here. It is a romantic spot, and it comes as no surprise that Sir Hugh Walpole should set *Judith Paris* in Watendlath. There is a car park and teas are served in Judith's home.

Retrace the route to the lakeshore and turn right for Keswick. More lovely woodland walks can be enjoyed from Great Wood car park at the foot of Walla Crag.

The road continues to the centre of Keswick, but you may like to finish the tour by turning left to the lakeside car park. A footpath leads the short distance to Friars Crag which offers a view considered by Ruskin to be one of the three finest in Europe. There is a memorial to Ruskin on the crag. Another fifteen-minute walk from the car park leads to a small wooded hill, Castle Crag, east of the B5289. From the top you can see the whole of the lake and its surrounding fells, the peaks of Scafell and Scafell Pike, and Criffel in Scotland. ■

• PLACES OF INTEREST •

Seatoller
The smooth green slate, still produced from the Honister quarries, splits cleanly to produce slates with a variety of commercial uses. Its attractive appearance makes it popular as ornamental

paving and for monuments. Before the road was made over the pass, the slates were taken by pack-horse to the west coast over the Sty Head Pass and round the west side of Great Gable to Wasdale Head . This route was also convenient for transporting smuggled goods and is known today as Moses Trod, after a quarryman who was also a notorious smuggler.

The Buttermere and Westmorland Green Slate Company welcome small groups of visitors if given twenty-four hours' notice. Telephone: Borrowdale (017687) 230.

Borrowdale
The beauty of this romantic valley appealed to seekers of the 'picturesque' as early as the eighteenth century, and it has remained one of the most popular areas in the Lake District. Perhaps the secret of this appeal lies in the valley's combination of awe-inspiring mountains and crags with gentle wooded scenery along the banks of the River Derwent. Johnny Wood has been given the status of a Site of Special Scientific Interest on account of its wealth of ferns and mosses.

Watendlath
Sir Hugh Walpole spent his later life at Brackenburn, a house in the Manesty Woods on the south-west shore of Derwent Water. He died there in 1941. He set the whole of his Lakeland family saga *The Herries Chronicle* in and around Borrowdale.

DERWENT WATER, THE NEWLANDS VALLEY AND LORTON VALE

44 MILES - 2 HOURS
START AND FINISH AT KESWICK

A circuit of Derwent Water with magnificent views begins this tour. The route turns south again down the Newlands valley, beloved by all readers of Beatrix Potter. A road over the high fells leads down to Crummock Water and the tour returns to Keswick along the eastern side of Bassenthwaite Lake.

Leave Keswick along the B5289 (Borrowdale road) heading south along the eastern shore of Derwent Water. The surrounding fells are beautifully wooded and, after about 1¹/₂ miles, a car park on the left at Great Wood provides an opportunity for some short walks to Walla Crag. **Pass the turning to Watendlath and continue along the lakeshore.** Kettlewell car park is on the right. If you wish to see the Lodore Falls, which are behind the Lodore Hotel, park here and turn right along the footpath on the other side of the road. The distance round is about 1 mile.

The valley widens at the southern end of the lake and the road runs close to the River Derwent as it approaches the bridge at Grange. Just before the bridge there is a parking area on the left. It is a good idea to leave your car here to explore the delightful little village of Grange on foot. Walk down the road and turn right over the double-arched stone bridge to the village, a cluster of cottages around a small green. A footpath leads south to one of the finest viewpoints in Borrowdale, Castle Crag. The distance round is about 2¹/₂ miles.

To continue the tour from the parking area, turn right A over the bridge to drive through Grange and head north along the western side of the lake. This road runs high giving glorious views for almost the whole length. After about 1 mile you pass a small pool in Manesty Woods and 'Brackenburn' on the left, the home of Sir Hugh Walpole from 1924 to 1941. Shortly after, Brandelhow Woods fringe the lakeshore. Owing to vigorous campaigning by Canon Rawnsley, the vicar of Crosthwaite, they were saved from development to become the first major property bought by the National Trust in 1902. The road kinks left to a car park at the foot of the long ridge of Cat Bells and from

---

• PLACES OF INTEREST •

Grange
As the name of the village suggests it was once an outlying farm for Furness Abbey. The Cistercians farmed their lands on the grange system using lay-brothers. Castle Crag is crowned by the remains of an Iron Age hill fort. 'Borrowdale' means 'valley of the fort'.

Lingholm
The gardens are particularly beautiful in spring and autumn. Plants and shrubs are on sale. Tearoom. Open 1 April–31 October daily 10–5. Telephone: Keswick (017687) 72003.

The Newlands Valley
A peaceful scene today, but in the sixteenth century the valley was the centre of a flourishing mining industry.

The Company of Mines Royal invited a German firm to 'search, dig, try, roast and melt all manner of mines and ores of gold, silver, copper and quicksilver' in the north of England, and the first mines were opened in the Newlands Valley. Miners' families settled on Vicar's or Derwent Isle, the largest of the lake's islands.

Copper, and a little silver and gold, were found. The ores were carried on waggons to be smelted at bloomeries around Derwent Water, notably at the nearest bay, Copperheap Bay, and at the forge by the River Greta near Keswick.

The mines became a royal monopoly, and during the Commonwealth the Parliamentary forces destroyed the forges and brought the industry to an end. Some miners were killed and others drafted into the army.

Traces of spoil heaps can still be seen in the valley grassed over by time.

here there are lakeside walks through Old Brandelhow and Brandelhow Park.

Follow the road to a Y-junction and take the right-hand road B signposted to Portinscale and Keswick. After a few yards, at the T-junction, bear right. In about ½ mile you will see the sign for Lingholm on the right. The large Victorian house is now the home of Viscount Rochdale, but the splendid gardens, noted for their rhododendrons and azaleas, are open for visitors. For many years the house was used for summer lets and Beatrix Potter stayed at Lingholm with her family on several occasions. She set *Squirrel Nutkin* at Lingholm. Her furry hero paddles his raft to Owl Island. Possibly she had St Herbert's Island in mind.

A few yards after the turning to Lingholm, turn sharp left C signposted to Ullock. The road curves round Swinside hill through Ullock to a T-junction. Turn left D to head south down

the Newlands Valley. Lush and green, this quiet vale tucked between the Derwent fells and the Cat Bells ridge, may lack some of the drama of Borrowdale but has a special charm all its own. **The Newlands Beck is on the right**

as the road passes the inn at Swinside to a T-junction. Turn right for the tiny hamlet of Stair which soon appears over a bridge on the right. Turn left over the bridge following the sign for

SCALE 1:250 000 OR 1 INCH TO 4 MILES *1 CM TO 2.5 KM*

79

Buttermere. The road runs along the side of the Derwent fells with the Newlands Beck threading the valley on the right. By the beck you will see the valley's other hamlet, Little Town. Here the daughter of the vicar of Newlands encountered Beatrix Potter's hedgehog, Mrs Tiggy Winkle, and the meeting inspired the book.

Pass the turning for Little Town and follow the road as it climbs the Derwent fells up **the valley of the Keskadale Beck.** After about 1 1/4 miles, just before the road hairpins left and drops to cross a bridge, you will see a small wood on the fellside on the right. This mat of low, twisted oaks is a rare survival of the primeval forest which once covered so much of the Lake District. The head of the valley is reached at Newlands Hause where there is a car park. **The road then descends steeply beside Mill Beck to meet the B5289** in Buttermere. This is an attractive village at the foot of the fells which overlooks the narrow strip of land separating Crummock Water and Buttermere (lake). The Fish Inn became famous in the nineteenth century as the home of the 'Beauty of Buttermere', a local girl who married a bigamist. He was also a forger and was hanged, but the 'Beauty' later re-married and all was well. Footpaths from car parks near the Fish Hotel lead

• PLACES OF INTEREST •

Keskadale
At the end of the last Ice Age, much of the Lake District was covered by a thin soil composed of gravel, sand, silt and boulder clay derived

mainly from volcanic rock. High rainfall leached out any calcium-containing minerals leaving an acid soil. On the high fells there were woods of birch or pine, but at lower levels native oak-woods covered the mountain sides. The tiny wood of sessile oaks (the acorns have no stalks) in the Keskadale valley on the side of Knott Rigg is one of the four surviving remnants of this native forest. The others are at Birkrigg, Naddle Forest and Swindale.

Opposite Knott Rigg, forming the southern boundary of the valley, are the oddly-named slopes of Robinson. The mountain is named after Richard Robinson who acquired the estate, and as this mountain had no name at the time he called it after himself.

Wythop Mill
A restored nineteenth-century sawmill powered by an 'overshot' water-wheel. There is an exhibition of wheel-wrights' and carpenters' tools. The mill has a coffee shop serving light lunches and teas. Open April–October Tuesday–Sunday 10.30–5.30. November–March Friday–Sunday 10.30–5.30. Telephone: Keswick (017687) 76394.

An ancient British sword, made of iron, jewelled at the hilt with a sheath of bronze, was found near Wythop Beck. Known as the Embleton Sword it can be seen in the British Museum.

Mirehouse
The house is open 30 March–30 October Sunday and Wednesday (also Friday in August) 2–4.30. Grounds daily 10.30–5.30. Telephone: Keswick (017687) 72287.

all round Buttermere and to a magnificent waterfall, Scale Force.

Turn right along the B5289 signposted to Lorton and Cockermouth, past a large car park on the left. The road continues close to the shore of Crummock Water. From the next car park, on the right at Hause Point, a footpath leads into the secluded valley of Rannerdale. Rowing boats can be hired from the next house you pass on the right of the road.

The road leaves the lake-shore to follow the River Cocker north along Lorton Vale. Keep to the B5289 through Low Lorton in the direction of Cockermouth. Pass the junction with the B5292 and, after about 1¼ miles, you meet a crossroads. Turn right E along the minor road signposted to Embleton and Wythop and continue for about 1¼ miles past a turning on the left. When the road turns left continue straight ahead F down the road for Wythop Mill. Pass a lane on the right and at the Y-junction take the left-hand

road to the mill. The road drops steeply to cross a bridge and bears left to the mill which is down an entry on the left. The working water-mill is open to the public.

Continue through Wythop Mill village. Ignore the road leading right. Keep on over the A66 to Embleton. At the T-junction in the village turn right for Dubwath. Pass the turning on the left for Higham Hall. Cumbria County Council hold weekend summer schools here. **Drive past the first sign for the B5291. A short distance further on in Dubwath village, as the road turns right, turn left along the B5291 signposted to Castle Inn.** You pass Ouse Bridge car park on the right which is a splendid place to stop for a lakeside picnic. Steps lead down to a small beach beside Bassenthwaite Lake. This peaceful lake is a national nature reserve with a wide variety of birdlife and a wealth of wild flowers. It is also the home of a rare fish, the vendace.

The road traces the north end of Bassenthwaite Lake

then continues east to meet the A591. Turn right to follow the eastern side of Bassenthwaite Lake following the signs for Keswick. Look for the signs for Dodd Wood car park after driving beside the lake for a little more than 3 miles. There is a picnic area and a converted saw mill houses a tearoom and a shop. Several waymarked trails lead from the car park. The green route leads to the top of Dodd Hill. There are wonderful views of the north-east fells and the Solway Firth from here.

From Dodd Wood you can also visit Mirehouse, an elegant manor beautifully situated close to the lakeside. In the nineteenth century it was the home of the Spedding family who welcomed many eminent literary figures. Among them was Alfred, Lord Tennyson, who composed the final verses of *Idylls of the King* (the death of Arthur) by the lake. Mirehouse is open to the public.

Keep to the A591 heading for Keswick and go over the A66 roundabout through Great Crosthwaite. Follow the A5271 as it turns left for Keswick town centre. ■

The heather-covered slopes of Melbreak tower above Crummock Water's western shore

THE DERWENT FELLS AND NORTHERN LAKELAND

53 MILES – 2¹/₂ HOURS
START AND FINISH AT COCKERMOUTH

Approached from the north, the Lake District fells form a dramatic contrast with the broad river valleys around Cockermouth. This tour visits Crummock Water, Buttermere and the western shores of Bassenthwaite Lake. It then heads north, to some less-frequented areas near the northern boundary of the National Park, giving wide views over the Solway Firth to the Scottish hills.

Leave Cockermouth heading south along the B5292. The road crosses the fertile farming land beside the River Cocker, but ahead rise the dramatic outlines of the Lakeland fells. **The road goes under the A66 and continues to a junction with the B5289. Bear right signed for Low Lorton, Loweswater and Buttermere, along the B5289, to follow the River Cocker as it winds along Lorton Vale.** The valley is lush and green, bordered by rounded fells. In Low Lorton the road dips close to the river and you pass Lorton Hall, a seventeenth-century house flanked by a fourteenth-century peel tower and a chapel.

The crags of Whiteside rise close to the road on the left as the B5289 follows the east bank of the river towards Crummock Water. **At the junction with the road for Loweswater turn left, keeping to the B5289 for Buttermere, and** continue to the northern end of Crummock Water. Lanthwaite car park is on the right. A few minutes' walk west from the car park brings you to beautiful Lanthwaite Wood with footpaths along the lakeshore. Close to the road, opposite the car park, are the embankments of an early settlement.

The road continues south close to the shore of Crummock Water. This lovely lake is hemmed between the sheer fells of

• PLACES OF INTEREST •

Cockermouth
Set in attractive countryside just north of the National Park boundary, Cockermouth is strategically placed at the confluence of the Cocker and the Derwent rivers. The Romans built their fort 'Derventio' just north of the present town. The castle, built in the angle between the two rivers, dates from the twelfth century and has had a turbulent history. In the centre of the town neat Georgian and Victorian houses are grouped around the market-place. Markets have been held here since the thirteenth century, and there is a market every Monday, preceded in the summer by the ringing of the Butter Bell. Leading west from the market square is the broad, tree-lined Main Street, flanked by pleasantly colour-washed houses. The most imposing is the birthplace of Cockermouth's most

famous former resident, William Wordsworth. This mid-eighteenth-century town house was owned by the wealthy Lowther family and was let to Wordsworth's father, Sir James Lowther's estate and law agent. William was born in 1770 and spent the first eight years of his life in Cockermouth. In *The Prelude* he recalls with pleasure the terraced walk behind the house and bathing in the nearby mill stream. The house is now the property of the National Trust and is open weekdays 1 April–31 October 11–5. Also Saturdays at varying times. Telephone: Cockermouth (01900) 824805.

On the north side of the market-place is the Doll and Toy Museum. Open 1 February–30 November daily 10–5. Telephone: (01900) 827606. The Cockermouth Festival is held during the third week in August.

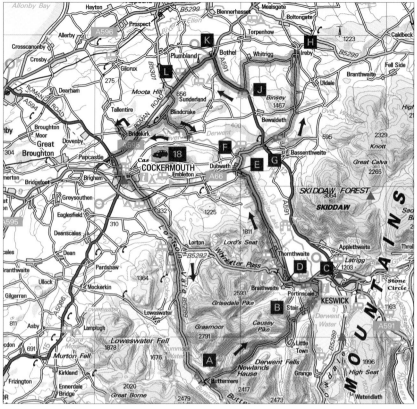

Melbreak to the west and Grasmoor to the east. The next car park, at the entrance to Rannerdale, provides an opportunity to explore this hidden valley which is carpeted with bluebells in early summer. **The road rounds Hause Point to descend to Buttermere village,** situated at the foot of Whiteless Pike, on the fertile strip of land between Crummock Water and Buttermere (lake). There is

parking close to the Fish Inn and footpaths lead around Buttermere (2½ miles) and to the highest waterfall in the Lake District, Scale Force (about 3 miles).

Cross the Mill Beck in Buttermere and follow the main road left uphill. Leave the B5289 as it bears right A and follow the minor road ahead signposted to Keswick, which climbs steeply between Knott Rigg and Robinson to

Newlands Hause. At the top there is a car park with splendid views. **The road descends beside the Keskadale Beck. After about 1½ miles the road hairpins right then dips to cross a beck.** Just after the road turns left to climb once more, look at the fellside on the left where a small oak wood clings to the almost sheer slope. This is a rare survival of the primeval forest that once covered all the lower mountain sides in the Lake District.

The road descends the Derwent fells for a little over 1 mile to the Newlands valley. Continue past the turning to Little Town. This is the small group of farms and cottages seen on the opposite side of Newlands Beck. **After about ½ mile, at the Y-junction, take the right-hand road B signposted to Portinscale. The road bears right to cross the bridge in Stair, the only other hamlet**

A quiet moment on the shore of Buttermere

83

A timeless lakeland scene beside Crummock Water

• PLACES OF INTEREST •

Low Lorton Hall
A refuge for Catholics during the Reformation, the house has priests' holes and secret passageways. Open by appointment. Telephone: Lorton (01900) 252.

Barf Rock
Legend relates that in 1783 the newly-appointed Bishop of Derry, after a few drinks in The Swan, betted his friends that he could ride his pony up the steep scree of Barf Fell. He succeeded, but the pony stumbled and the bishop was killed. He is said to be buried at the foot of the scree near the rock known as 'The Clerk'. The landlord of The Swan has the rock white-washed annually.

Thornthwaite Galleries
There is a craft shop and a tearoom. Open March–October Wednesday–Monday 10.30–5. November Friday–Sunday 10.30–5. Telephone: Braithwaite (017687) 78248.

Ireby
Markets have been held in Ireby since the village was granted its charter in 1237.

John Keats visited the Sun Inn in 1818 and this London-born Cockney enjoyed watching the local people make merry. He describes the dancing in a letter in language almost as lively. 'They kickit and jumpit with mettle extraordinary and whiskit and friskit and toed it and go'd it...' He concludes, 'This is what I like better than scenery.'

Bridekirk
The village takes its name from St Bridget to whom the church is dedicated. The font was carved by Richard, the Carver of Durham, who has inscribed his name on one of the sides in runic letters. On the other sides are intricately patterned scrolls and scenes from the Baptism of Christ and the expulsion of Adam and Eve from the Garden of Eden.

in the valley, and meets a T-junction. Turn left for Swinside. In Swinside the road divides. Keep on past the inn for Portinscale. At the Y-junction bear left for a few yards to a T-junction and bear left again for Portinscale.

In Portinscale village bear left **C** to meet the A66. Turn left for Cockermouth. In a little more than 1 mile leave the A66 and bear left along the B5292 to Braithwaite. Take the first turning on the right **D** to Thornthwaite, a small village to the left of the road. The road runs towards the A66 but, before meeting it, bears left to run almost parallel before entering Thornthwaite. A sign indicates Thornthwaite Galleries housed in a two-hundred-year-old building. Fine examples of traditional crafts are among the many unusual items exhibited in the galleries.

The road runs along the foot of Thornthwaite Forest and passes the seventeenth-century Swan

Hotel on the right. Powter Howe car park is just past the hotel. Across the road, high up on the fell, is a whitewashed pinnacle of rock known as the Bishop of Barf. It bears a faint resemblance to a man in a white surplice!

Follow the road for another ³/₄ mile to the junction with the A66 where you will see Woodend car park and picnic place. Bear left to follow the A66 close to the western shore of Bassenthwaite Lake. Keep to the A66 past a junction on the left, then leave the main road and turn right E along the B5291 for Dubwath. After a few yards the road divides. Take the right-hand road (B5291) which returns to the lakeside then bears left beside the River Derwent. Turn right F, signposted to Castle Inn and Bothel. Cross the bridge over the river, keeping to the B5291 as it traces the northern end of the lake then runs east to a T-junction. Bear right for a few yards then left G for Ireby. After about 2 miles bear left to leave the main road following the sign for Ireby. At the first crossroads as you enter this pleasant market town turn left H

signed for High Ireby and Whitrigg. You pass Ireby's old market cross on the left. The road bears left to a Y-junction. Continue along the right-hand road for Whitrigg. This follows the northern boundary of the National Park over Humble Jumble Gill past Snittlegarth Park. **Pass a turning to Whitrigg on the right and continue for Bassenthwaite.** You have marvellous views now west and north over the Solway Firth to the Scottish hills beyond Annan and Dumfries. To the south rise the lonely slopes of Skiddaw.

Shortly after the turning to Whitrigg the road turns left. In about ³/₄ mile you will see the outlines of Caermote Roman Fort on the right. **Continue to meet the A591 and turn right J for Bothel.** The road leaves the National Park to cross the Bothel Beck and approach the village. **Just after entering Bothel the A591 meets the A595. Turn left K along the A595 in the direction of Cockermouth.** The A595 soon becomes ruler-straight as it follows the line of a Roman road marking the boundary of the National Park. **Pass the road to Arkleby on the right (B5301) and turn left L down the next road**

for Blindcrake. Drive into the village and turn left following the sign for Isel. Follow the road for more than a mile as it descends south into the Derwent valley towards Isel Bridge. Just before the bridge turn right down the track to Isel church. There is a large parking and turning area here. John Betjeman has captured the atmosphere of this small church with its simple Norman chancel arch in the quote you will see inside. 'A perfect harmony of man and Nature – a setting for Jane Austen.'

Retrace the route to Blindcrake. Turn left at the junction in the village and drive through Redmain to rejoin the A595. Turn left for Cockermouth and, after about ¹/₂ mile, turn right for Bridekirk. Drive through the village and, when the road bends left, keep straight on towards Tallentire. There is room to park by the church on the left. It was rebuilt in 1870 preserving its original beautifully-carved twelfth-century font.

Retrace your route to the A595 and turn right for Cockermouth. At the round-about bear left along the A5086 to cross the Derwent and enter the town. ■

Homely Isel church in its perfect setting beside the Derwent

MARYPORT, ENNERDALE AND LOWESWATER

56 MILES – 2½ HOURS
START AND FINISH AT COCKERMOUTH

This tour begins by heading north-west to the Cumbrian coast to enjoy the magnificent views over the Solway Firth near Maryport before turning south to visit two of the Lake District's quieter lakes – Ennerdale Water, dominated by the great peak of Pillar, and Loweswater, calm and spacious between gently rolling fells.

Drive west along Main Street in Cockermouth (B5292). Cross the junction with the A5086 and continue along Crown Street (A5086). Turn right **A** following the sign for Carlisle. Cross Derwent Bridge and continue along Goat Road. At the roundabout keep straight on heading north up Goat Brow and follow the A595 signed for Carlisle. After about ½ mile bear left along the minor road signposted to Bridekirk. At the Y-junction bear right. Bear left at the next junction to enter the village. Leave the main road as it turns left and keep straight on

B, signposted to Tallentire. Continue to Bridekirk church. There is room to park here. The church was built in 1870 in neo-Norman style, but has retained an exquisitely-carved twelfth-century font. Beasts, flowers and tiny figures form patterned friezes around scenes from the Baptism of Christ, the expulsion from the Garden of Eden and, possibly, a portrait of the sculptor himself, Richard, the Carver of Durham, who signs his name in runic letters.

Continue past the church to a T-junction. This takes you through pleasantly-undulating countryside with wide views. Turn right **C**, signposted

to Gilcrux and Bullgill, to drive through Tallentire. The attractive village is sheltered by the rounded slopes of Tallentire Hill. Follow the principal road through the village, which turns right past the Hall, then left and right again to resume its original heading to a junction. Bear left **D**, and continue for just over 1 mile. Ignore a turning on the left, and shortly you come to a Y-junction. Take the left-hand road for Bullgill. The road dips into the valley of the River Ellen, crosses the river and the railway. When you meet the A596 at Crosby Villa turn left along the A596 signed for

Beside the harbour entrance at Maryport

Workington. You enter Crosby village after 1 mile. Drive through the village for about ¼ mile then turn right **E** along the minor road for Crosscanonby. Over the Scad Beck, just before the road bears right, you will see the mainly twelfth-century church on the left. This area, close to the Roman road running beside the Solway Firth to the fort at Maryport, is rich in Roman remains, and the builders of this small church have made good use of these in their stonework. There is a beautifully-carved Saxon cross shaft and some fine early eighteenth-century woodwork.

The road turns left in Crosscanonby to the shore of the Solway Firth and meets the B5300, which follows the course of the Roman road. There is a car park here, wide sandy beaches and splendid views.

Turn left to follow the B5300 past the site of a small Roman fort at Brown Rigg to the junction with the A596. Bear right along the A596 for Maryport. Just past the church, turn left along the A594 F to cross the River Ellen and the railway heading for Cockermouth. Ignore all side roads and keep to the A594 as it runs south-east to the pretty village of Dovenby. About ¾ mile after Dovenby turn right at the crossroads G in the direction of Great Broughton. Continue for about 2 miles to the next crossroads. Turn left H, and keep straight on following the signs for Cockermouth, over a road to cross the River Derwent and meet the A66. Turn left and follow the A66 south of Cockermouth. At the roundabout keep to the A66 signed for Keswick. Pass the junction on the left with the A5086 but, shortly after, turn right J along the A5086 signed for Egremont heading south. After ¾ mile you will see

Moorland Close on the right, where Fletcher Christian, leader of the mutiny on the *Bounty,* was born in 1764.

The road now runs past a lane leading to Eaglesfield, the birthplace in 1766 of John Dalton, formulator of the atomic theory. John Dalton House is marked by a plaque above the door.

To see the exterior of his house make a detour by turning right down the lane for Eaglesfield. Drive into the village and, when the main road bends left at a Y-junction, turn right to follow a narrow road past the post office. The road bends sharply left and John Dalton's birthplace is the black and white house on the right. **To return to the A5086, follow the road round the left bend to a T-junction. Turn left and continue past a road on the**

John Dalton House in Eaglesfield

left bearing a little right following the sign for Deanscales. At the Y-junction take the left-hand road signposted to Mosser which rejoins the A5086. Turn right following the sign for Lamplugh.

Continue along the A5086 for about 3 miles. Just after the sign for Mockerkin a layby on the left affords a good view of

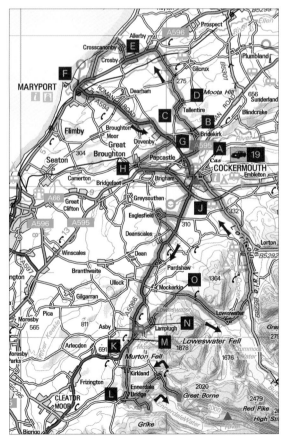

The coast near Crosscanonby, looking across the sands of the Solway Firth to the Scottish hills

Mockerkin Tarn, a charming little lake with ducks and waterlilies. **Continue for another 3 miles then turn left K along the road for Kirkland. Follow the road through Kirkland to Ennerdale Bridge, beside the River Ehen as it flows out of Ennerdale Water. Turn left for Ennerdale Water and, when the road forks, take the right-hand road for the lake to the car park close to its western shore.** Footpaths to the lakeshore lead to delightful picnic places

and you can enjoy one of the most magnificent views in the Lake District. North-east rise the mountains of the High Stile range. South-west the Pillar group of peaks with the great Pillar Rock dominates the lakeside. Ahead, the dale is closed by Great Gable.

Waymarked trails around the lake can be started from the car park at Bowness Knott on the north shore, but the access road is very narrow. **To reach this car park, retrace the route from the park on the western**

shore to the fork in the road and turn right. Ignore the first sign on the right for Ennerdale Water (fishermen only) and keep ahead signed for Croasdale. Keep ahead, past the turning for Croasdale. Follow the signs for Ennerdale Water for about 2¹/₂ miles to Bowness Knott car park and picnic place. Leaflets give details of three possible trails: The Nine Becks Walk (9 miles) and two shorter trails of between 2 to 3 miles –

• PLACES OF INTEREST •

Maryport
Situated at the mouth of the River Ellen on the Solway Firth, Maryport was once a busy coaling port and involved with the iron industry. Today other industries have developed including plastics and engineering. But it is still an attractive coastal resort with an interesting harbour and sandy beaches. It is a planned town built on a grid pattern, but there has been a settlement here since the time of the Romans. They built a fort, Alauna, the remains of which are just to the north of the present

town. This was one of a chain of defensive positions built along the coast of the Solway Firth to protect the flank of Hadrian's Wall which ended at Bowness on the Solway. Interesting finds, including altars, can be seen in the Senhouse Roman Museum. Opening times vary. Telephone: Maryport (01900) 816168

Old ships are often berthed in the harbour and visitors are welcomed aboard three steam-powered tugs. Facing the harbour is the information centre and on the floor above is the Maryport

Maritime Museum. Here you can find a wealth of nautical equipment, pictures, models and paintings telling the story of Maryport's links with the sea, including a copy of Captain Bligh's log-book open on the fateful day of the mutiny. There are links also with the White Star Line and the Titanic. Opening times vary. Telephone: Maryport (01900) 813738.

Motte Hill stands in a loop of the Ellen. Follow the short footpath to the top to watch the sun set beyond the Isle of Man.

Ennerdale

The village of Ennerdale Bridge, the gateway to the most westerly of the lakes, is surrounded by magnificent scenery. Wordsworth visited the church in 1799 (the present church was built later in 1857) and set his poem *The Brothers* in Ennerdale. It is based on the story of a shepherd who lost his life on Pillar Rock. The upper part of the valley has been heavily forested, but Pillar Rock still rises, as Wordsworth describes it, *like a column from the vale*.

As there are no roads round Ennerdale Water it has remained remote and peaceful. It is a haven for many rare birds including peregrine, great crested grebe and osprey. In 1980 the lake was threatened by plans to raise the water level to provide greater supplies for the coastal industries. This was vigorously opposed by the National Trust and other responsible organisations who succeeded in preserving the lake and its attractive shoreline.

The Ennerdale Show is held at Bowness Knott on the last Wednesday in August.

Loweswater

Loweswater is unique in that it falls eastwards towards the long valley of Crummock Water and Buttermere. All the other lakes and their valleys run outward from the central fells. The movement of the great glaciers that produced this effect distributed the debris that

became a rich fertile soil around Loweswater's shores.

The small farms that flourish here have remained almost unchanged through the centuries and contribute to the special charm of this lovely lake. The Loweswater and Brackenthwaite Show is held on the third Thursday in September.

---

the Smithy Beck Trail and the Liza Path. All offer splendid views and historic interest.

Retrace your route to Ennerdale Bridge. Continue retracing the route by turning right just before the bridge in the direction of Kirkland, signposted to Loweswater and Cockermouth. Drive through Kirkland village to rejoin the A5086. Turn right and continue for about ¼ mile, then take the first road on the right signposted to Lamplugh Green. Bear left at the junction for Lamplugh village following the sign for Loweswater. Continue through Lamplugh and turn right for Loweswater. At the T-junction bear right to the western shore of this pleasant 'leafy' lake. There are car parks here. A short walk takes you to beautiful Holme Wood on the southern shore where there is a waterfall and seats.

Follow the road as it traces the northern shore of the lake. The road continues to the foot of Lorton Vale, but it is worth making a short detour left to Loweswater village. From the church there is a magnificent view down Crummock Water which, unlike Loweswater, is penned between sheer mountain slopes with Melbreak to the west and Grasmoor to the east.

Rejoin the main road bearing right to cross the River Cocker to Scale Bridge car park. From the car park short walks through Lanthwaite Wood lead round the northern shore of Crummock Water.

The road turns north along the east side of the River Cocker through Lorton Vale. Keep on for Lorton to meet the B5289. Bear left to continue north for Low Lorton and follow the signs for Cockermouth. After Low Lorton the road runs close to the river then bears right to a T-junction. Turn left, keeping to the B5289, to meet the B5292. Turn left along the B5292 which continues north over the A66 to the centre of Cockermouth. ■

Remote Ennerdale Water is framed by magnificent mountains

WESTERN LAKELAND AND WASDALE

70 MILES- 3¹/₂ HOURS
START AND FINISH AT COCKERMOUTH

This exciting tour heads south over remote fells giving wide sea views to the coast at Seascale and then turns east to run along the shore of the National Park's most dramatic lake, Wast Water. Historic interest includes the ruins of Calder Abbey and the famous Gosforth Cross. The return route offers an opportunity to explore the quiet shores of Ennerdale Water.

Leave Cockermouth heading south along the A5086. At the junction with the A66 turn left for about 200 yards (183 m) then turn right, heading south again, still following the A5086. Keep to the main road for about 7 miles, past Mockerkin Tarn. The road runs past **Lamplugh Cross**. After ¹/₄ mile, leave the main road and turn left **A** for **Kirkland. Keep straight on over the crossroads in Kirkland and continue for Ennerdale Bridge.** Splendid views of the high fells open ahead, and on the left you look down on the wooded vale of Ennerdale Water.

Bear right at the fork in Ennerdale Bridge, then right again to cross the bridge over the River Ehen. You pass the church on the right which replaced an earlier building visited by Wordsworth. He set his poem *The Brothers* in Ennerdale. **Continue for a little more than ¹/₂ mile, then turn left B along a fellside road signposted to Calder Bridge and Gosforth.** The road climbs to give wide views over the Ennerdale fells and west to the coast and Sellafield. In less than 1 mile the road climbs Scarny Brow and crosses a cattle-grid. A little further on rising from a plateau on the left you will see Kinniside Stone Circle. The stones are impressive in their lonely moorland setting, but there are doubts as to their authenticity. It is said that they were arranged there by a local archaeologist merely as an example of how a prehistoric stone circle should look!

Shortly after, the steep slopes of the inappropriately-named Flat Fell rise on the right above Nannycatch Beck. There are parking areas beside the road and a short walk over the grass reveals

A hidden valley - Nannycatch Gate

a hidden valley where three streams meet beneath Raven Crag. This lovely valley, Nannycatch Gate, tops the list of Alfred Wainwright's favourite out-of-the-way places.

Follow the road as it runs south over the fells giving splendid views over the water to the Isle of Man. **When the road forks, take the left-hand road signposted to Calder Bridge, to a T-junction. Turn left for a few yards, then left again** **C** **down the road signposted to Prior Scales.** After about 100 yards (91 m) there is roadside parking from where you can see the ruins of Calder Abbey, built of red St Bees sandstone, in the valley. For a closer view take the footpath signposted to Calder Bridge which runs past the ruins. **Return to the junction** **C** **and continue straight on to meet the A595 at Calder Bridge.**

If you would like to visit Sellafield, turn right for a few hundred yards then turn left following the signs for the visitors centre.

Turn left along the A595 for Gosforth and Barrow to cross Calder Bridge. After ³/₄ mile you will see the lane to Ponsonby Old Hall on the left. The farm, which contains buildings dating back to the thirteenth century, is open for visitors and children can stroke and feed the friendly animals.

Keep along the A595 for another 1¹/₄ miles and take the first road on the right (B5344) for Seascale. The seafront of this small resort has retained its Victorian charm. **Drive through the village and under the railway to the seafront.** There is a car park on the right.

Follow the B5344 as it turns left along the coast to cross the railway and continue towards Drigg on the estuary of the River Irt. Drigg is famous for its sand dunes. **To get close to them turn right just before the**

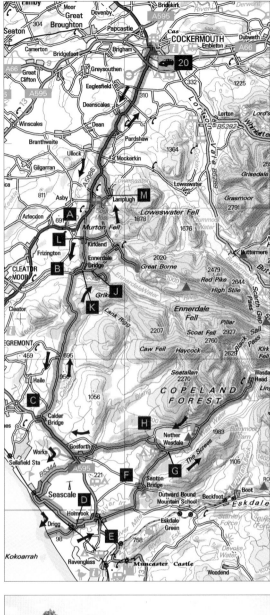

The ruins of Calder Abbey

village  and follow the road to the car park. South of the village the Ravenglass Gullery and Nature Reserve has been established on the dunes at the confluence of the Irt and the Esk. It is well-known for its rich wildlife which includes a large black-headed gull colony, terns, peregrine and merganser. Rare natterjack toads breed here.

Follow the B5344 to meet the A595 at Holmrook. Turn right signed for Barrow to cross the bridge over the River Irt and take the next minor road on the left **E** for Santon Bridge. In a little less than 1 mile turn left following the sign for Irton Cross and St Paul's Church. The track leads to a large parking area. At the far side of the churchyard among the gravestones stands a ninth-century Anglian cross in an excellent state of preservation.

Return to the road which follows the eastern side of the River Irt to a T-junction. Turn left for a few yards, then, before the bridge, turn right **F** for Wasdale. The road runs north through beautiful wooded fells to cross the river at Forest Bridge. Immediately afterwards the road divides. Take the right-hand road **G** signposted to Wasdale Head to a T-junction and bear right again following the sign for Wasdale Head. After a descent through a maze of dry-stone walls one of the most magnificent views in Lakeland opens before you. Ahead lies Wast Water, walled to the south by awe-inspiring screes. The head of the lake is closed by the mighty peaks of Scafell, Scafell Pike and Great Gable.

Follow the road along the lakeshore to the car park near the hotel at Wasdale Head. You will pass several car parks by the waterside before reaching Wasdale Head. A short walk signposted from here leads to the tiny Church of St Olaf which has many links with climbers. The pack-horse bridge would have been crossed frequently during the seventeenth and eighteenth centuries by pack trains carrying slate from Honister and graphite from Borrowdale to the coast at Drigg and returning with imported tobacco, spirits and coal.

Retrace your route to the turning to Santon Bridge at **G**, but do not turn left. Instead, carry straight on for Gosforth through Nether Wasdale. At the junction bear left **H** for Gosforth. Continue for 2 miles to a T-junction. Turn left to enter Gosforth village. St Mary's Church is on the right. Turn right just past the church to a parking area. The church contains relics of the early Viking settlers and in the churchyard you will see the famous Gosforth Cross.

Continue past the church and bear right at the T-junction. A few yards further on take the right-hand road at the fork and bear right to meet the A595. Turn right along the main road to retrace the route turning right in Calder Bridge for Ennerdale, left at **C** for just a few yards, then right to recross the fells towards Ennerdale Bridge. At the T-junction turn right to cross a bridge. Turn right again when you come to the next T-junction to cross Ennerdale Bridge.

Leave the earlier route here. Do not turn left but continue straight ahead for Ennerdale Water. When the road forks **J** you might like to make a detour along the right-hand road. This runs to a car park close to the waterside giving access to walks and picnic places.

Return to the fork at **J**.

Sheer screes tumble into Wast Water's south-eastern shore

Calder Abbey

The abbey was founded in 1134 by monks from Savigny who later adopted the Cistercian rule. During the Border Wars the monks were forced to flee and the abbey became the property of the Abbot of Furness. The remains include part of the tower and the chancel, a west doorway and some bays of the north aisle.

Sellafield Visitor Centre

The centre provides a journey into the nuclear age for all the family with computer games and quizzes, multi-screen presentations and life-size working models. Open 1 April–31 October daily 10–6. Rest of year daily 10–4. Telephone: Seascale (019467) 27027.

Ponsonby Farm Park

The Farm Park is in the grounds of Ponsonby Old Hall which is a private residence. It is a working dairy farm with an extensive collection of rare farm animals. For children there is a pets' corner and play areas. Tearoom and shop. Open Easter week, 1 May–30 September Tuesday–Sunday 10.30–5. Telephone: Beckermet (01946) 841426.

Ravenglass Gullery and Nature Reserve

The gullery contains the largest population of black-headed gulls in Europe. It is owned by Muncaster Castle but managed by Cumbria County Council. Access is by permit which can be obtained from the County Estate and Valuer, Arroyo Block, The Castle, Carlisle. Telephone: Carlisle (01228) 23456.

Irton

'Tun' is Old English for a farmstead, and it is likely that there was an Anglo-Saxon settlement here during the brief period between the Celts and the coming of the Vikings from the Isle of Man.

Ancient trackways converge at the isolated Church of St Paul which was rebuilt in the eighteenth century. In the churchyard is a stunning ninth-century red sandstone cross, possibly erected by a wealthy Saxon. It is ornamented by elaborately-carved knotwork of Irish origin. The church is included on the Cumbria Christian Heritage Trail.

Gosforth

The tenth-century cross in St Mary's churchyard has an extraordinary claim to fame. 14 feet (4.2 m) high, the wheel cross stands at the top of a pillar carved at the base to represent the bark of the sacred ash tree. The carvings on both sides of the cross represent the triumph of good over evil, but one side depicts the crucifixion of Christ and the other scenes from Norse mythology. The new Norse settlers were taking no chances with regard to religion!

Lamplugh

The Church of St. Michael is well-known for its gargoyles and double bell-cote. But the village is also famous for a perfect pick-me-up after a walk on the fells, Lamplugh Pudding. Hot spiced ale is added to oats or crushed biscuits with the addition of dried fruit and brown sugar.

Another detour could be made here by turning right and driving for 2¹/₂ miles to the car park by the lakeside at Bowness Knott. (Beware, the road is very narrow!)Leaflets give details of forest trails.

Return to Ennerdale Bridge. Just before the bridge turn right K signposted to Cockermouth to head towards Kirkland. At the crossroads in Kirkland turn right L signposted to Croasdale. When you come to a T-junction turn left to follow the road curving round the foot of Lamplugh Fell. At the next T-junction turn right signposted to Loweswater. Drive past the church in Lamplugh and keep straight on M to meet the A5086. Turn right along the A5086 to return to Cockermouth. ■

Irton Cross

USEFUL ADDRESSES AND INFORMATION

For information on daily events and weather forecasts

North
95.6 FM 756 AM
West
95.6 FM 1458 AM
South
96.1 FM 837 AM
Kendal
95.2 FM
Windermere
104.2 FM

Lake District Weather Forecast
Tel: (019662) 5151

National Park Information Centres

Bowness Bay
Tel: (015394) 42895
Coniston
Tel: (015394) 41533
Glenridding
Tel: (017684) 82414
Grasmere
Tel: (015394) 35245
Hawkshead
Tel: (015394) 36525
Keswick
Tel: (017687) 72803
Pooley Bridge
Tel: (017684) 86530
Seatoller
Tel: (017687) 77294
Waterhead
Tel: (015394) 32729

National Trust Information Centres

Ambleside, Bridge House

Keswick, Boat Landings
Tel: Keswick (017687) 73780

Grasmere, opposite the church
Tel: Grasmere (015394) 35621

Fell Foot Park, Newby Bridge
Tel: Newby Bridge (015395) 31273

National Trust Regional Office

The National Trust
The Hollens, Grasmere, Ambleside,
Cumbria LA22 9QZ.
Tel: Grasmere (015394) 35599

Tourist Information Centres
Opening times vary – check by telephone

Ambleside
Church Street, Ambleside,
Cumbria LA22 OBT.
Tel: Ambleside (015394) 32582

Appleby-in-Westmorland
Moot Hall, Boroughgate,
Appleby-in-Westmorland,
Cumbria CA16 6XD.
Tel: Appleby (017683) 51177

Bowness-on-Windermere
Glebe Road, Bowness-on-
Windermere, Cumbria LA23 3HJ.
Tel: Windermere (015394) 42895

Cockermouth
Town Hall, Cockermouth,
Cumbria CA13 9NP.
Tel: Cockermouth (019000) 822634

Coniston
16 Yewdale Road, Coniston, Cumbria
LA21 8DU.
Tel: Coniston (015394) 41533

Grasmere
Redbank Road, Grasmere,
Cumbria LA22 9SW.
Tel: Grasmere (015394) 35245

Hawkshead
Main Car Park, Hawkshead, Cumbria
LA22 0NT.
Tel: Hawkshead (015394) 36525

Kendal
Town Hall, Highgate, Kendal,
Cumbria LA9 4DL.
Tel: Kendal (01539) 725758

Keswick
Moot Hall, Market Square, Keswick,
Cumbria CA12 4JR.
Tel: Keswick (017687) 72645

Kirkby Lonsdale
24 Main Street, Kirkby Lonsdale,
Cumbria LA6 2AE.
Tel: Kirkby Lonsdale (015242)
71437

Maryport
Maryport Maritime Museum,
1 Senhouse Street, Maryport,
Cumbria CA15 6AB.
Tel: Maryport (01900) 813738

Penrith
Middlegate, Penrith,
Cumbria CA11 7PT.
Tel: Penrith (01768) 67466

Pooley Bridge
The Square, Pooley Bridge, Penrith,
Cumbria CA10 2NW.
Tel: Pooley Bridge (017684) 86530

Ravenglass
Ravenglass and Eskdale Railway
Station, Ravenglass,
Cumbria CA18 1SW.
Tel: Ravenglass (01229) 717278

Seatoller
Seatoller Barn, Borrowdale, Keswick,
Cumbria CA12 5XN.
Tel: Borrowdale (017687) 77294

Ullswater
Main Car Park, Glenridding, Penrith,
Cumbria CA11 0PA.
Tel: Glenridding (017684) 82414

Ulverston
Coronation Hall, County Square,
Ulverston, Cumbria LA12 7LZ.
Tel: Ulverston (01229) 587120

Waterhead
Main Car Park, Waterhead,
Ambleside, Cumbria LA22 0EN.
Tel: Ambleside (015394) 32729

Windermere
Victoria Street, Windermere,
Cumbria LA23 1AD.
Tel: Windermere (015394) 46499

Other useful organisations

The Council for the Protection of Rural England
25 Buckingham Palace Road
London SW1W OPP.
Tel: (0171) 976 6433

The Countryside Commission
John Dower House, Crescent Place,
Cheltenham,
Gloucestershire GL50 3RA.
Tel: Cheltenham (01242) 521381

Cumbria Tourist Board
Ashleigh, Holly Road, Windermere,
Cumbria LA23 2AQ.
Tel: Windermere (015394) 44444

The Forestry Commission
Information Branch,
231 Corstorphine Road
Edinburgh EH12 7AT.
Tel: Edinburgh (0131) 334 0303

Friends of the Lake District
3 Yard 77, Highgate, Kendal, Cumbria
LA9 4ED.
Tel: Kendal (01539) 720788

The Lake District National Park Visitor Centre
Brockhole, Windermere,
Cumbria OA23 1LJ.
Tel: Windermere (015394) 46601

Council for National Parks
246 Lavender Hill,
London SW11 1LJ.
Tel: 0171 924 4077

Ordnance Survey
Romsey Road, Maybush
Southampton SO16 4GU.
Tel: Southampton (01703) 792912

INDEX